This Is My Story

Growing in Grace

by Glen O. Suiter

To Bill Seal
my long time family friend
Glen O Suiter
11/17/21

DORRANCE
PUBLISHING CO
EST. 1920
PITTSBURGH, PENNSYLVANIA 15238

Dorrance Publishing Co
585 Alpha Drive
Pittsburgh, PA 15238
Visit our website at *www.dorrancebookstore.com*

ISBN: 978-1-4809-9353-2
eISBN: 978-1-4809-9360-0

Acknowledgment

It is with great appreciation that I acknowledge the work that my wife has devoted to editing this manuscript. She has spend many hours reading and rereading, correcting and recorrecting. My deepest respect and gratefulness go to my wife, Donna Suiter, for her work.

Contents

My Early Years

The purpose of my writing is so that my children and grandchildren will have something to look at and laugh or cry, however the mood hits them. As I reflect on the direction my life has taken, I think of the song "It Took a Miracle," and I believe that it has been a miracle how God has brought me to the place of fully accepting who I am.

It took a Miracle to put the Stars in space
It took a miracle to put the world in place
But when He saved my soul cleansed and ***made me whole***
It took a miracle of love and grace

I entered into this world on a hot summer day about noon on the seventh day of August 1935. My parents were living on a small farm near Collbran, Colorado. I was the seventh child born into the Joseph William (JW) and Lulu Fay (Fry) Suiter family. By this time, two girls and four boys had already taken their respective places in the family. I was given the names Glen, after a Nazarene evangelist Glen Griffin that Dad thought a lot of, and Oliver, after my grandfather, Oliver Parry Fry.

Opal commented on the day of my birth.

> *I remember when Glen was born. I was sent to get the midwife. She lived about a mile down the road & then a long lane to her house. The lane followed the pasture, which was fenced, but whoever heard of a fence keeping a bull in? I ran the whole way, scared out of my wits! But the reward was a baby brother!*

There would be another girl and two boys to round out the total number of siblings to an even ten. My older brother Jim used to say that the Suiters were like horse manure and blackberry bushes—they were everywhere. It sure seemed that way. We always had a crowd around our home, especially at suppertime. Our table was always surrounded by a whole host of people—family and friends.

My older sister, Polly, tells me that I was always hungry. Apparently Mother had run out of milk and I was suffering from malnutrition. She said that I tried to nurse on anything and anyone that I could get my mouth on. I guess I cried a lot and probably was a real pain to everyone, especially on the long trip to Oregon in 1936.

My siblings consisted of, in order of birth, a sister, Margaret Pauline, we always called her Polly; next a brother, Lewis Alfred, mostly known as Louie; then another sister, Opal May. I remembered her because, when Dad would call her in the morning, he would always call, "Opal May, time to get up." I am told that Polly and Lewis gave Opal a hard time as kids; they liked to play tricks on her. Joseph Robert followed Opal, and soon after came Jimmie Leon. Samuel Everett brought up the rear to complete the first six. I will fill in the last three in the proper time as they arrived.

I am told that I arrived in the middle of the Great Depression, and making a living was very difficult. Dad was never one to sit and see his family suffer if he could do something about it. When Dad decided to move the family out west to Oregon, some thought that he had lost his good sense. Lewis told me that a lady said to Dad one day, "You know, Joe, a rolling stone gathers no moss," and Dad responded with, "Yes, and a sitting hen never gets fat."

The Woodruffs, friends of the family from Kansas, had moved to Oregon. They wrote to Dad and said that there was work and plenty of opportunity out in Oregon. So in the summer of 1936, Dad loaded the family up in a 1929 Chevy truck and headed for the promise land—Oregon. We arrived in Oregon in the early fall of 1936 and settled around Roseburg.

On July 8,1937, Merle Lavern arrived. This gave the family their third girl. Merle and I were to become the best of friends, at least until I started school. I don't remember her not being there and many of my early adventures included her as my partner. It seemed like I was always saying, "Come on, Merle, let's do..." whatever I happened to think of, and off we would go.

There are a few events that I remember happened when I was between three and four-and-a-half. One event that stands out to me was when a big red rooster jumped on my head. I don't know how old I was at the time. I would guess around three. We had some company visiting, and as they were leaving, we were all out in yard saying goodbye when that rooster ran at me and jumped on my head. This scared the life out of me, and of course I started to cry.

What I don't remember is what Polly told me later. Polly related how that rooster had been chasing all of the kids, and when he jumped on me, she said that she had had enough. She told me that she chased that rooster and he ran way up under the house; he knew he had gone too far that time. Polly said that she crawled in after him and dragged him out from under the house and executed him right then and there. She said Dad never said a word to her about killing that rooster.

While living in the Roberts Creek area where the rooster event took place, I remember a few other things that happened, although I don't know in what order. Dad had found a bee tree and robbed the honey from it. I remember him taking the old truck and driving up to the tree. It was a big oak that had a hollow in it where the bees had built their nest. Dad and the older boys took a crosscut saw and cut the tree down so they could get the honey out.

Lewis told me later that Dad had a way of following the bees to the tree. Louie said that Dad would watch the bees get their fill of pollen from the flowers, then he would watch them to see which direction they would fly. He would watch them at different places along the route from the flowers to the tree, and that is how he knew where the bee tree was.

On another occasion, the older boys and I were out at the barn, and they decided it would be fun to give me a ride in a wagon. We had a little red wagon, and they tied the wagon to the horse's tail. This worked great until the horse turned down hill, at which time the wagon ran into the horse's heels. The horse's response was to kick at the wagon, when this happened, the wagon was kicked over. I was under the wagon and was dragged until the boys could catch the horse and get me out. I was not hurt, most likely just scared. Later I was relating this story to my brother Jim, and he confirmed that it was Joe who instigated that event.

I am not sure when we moved, but we moved to a little house east of Roseburg to Glide, Oregon. That is where I really begin finding that life could be exciting. I enjoyed many adventures while we lived there although I don't think we lived there very long. Most of my memory revolves around the home where we lived, and I was not one to sit still for long. I am not sure of the order of events, but most of them happened in the spring of 1940. I turned five that August.

I remember the family playing a lot of games and pranks. We played "Annie, Annie Over." The boys would throw the ball over the roof of the shed in back of the house, and yell, "Annie, Annie Over." They would try to catch the ball as it rolled off of the roof then throw it back and yell, "Annie, Annie Over." I don't remember everything we did, but there was never a dull moment. In the evenings, we would come together, and Polly would play the piano and Lewis played the guitar. We would sing and tell stories.

At Christmas, we made our tree decorations by stringing popcorn and making colored paper chains. We would cut the colored paper into strips and glue the ends together using flour and water for glue. Our trees were highly decorated. Along with the fun times, there were hard times also. Dad was struggling to provide enough for us to live on, and somehow I knew that times were hard for us. I will talk about that later.

As a four-almost-five-year-old, I was an adventurous boy determined to make my own place in the world. I can't say why I felt the way I did, but I know that I was set on exploring my world and making my contribution to the family. Some of my most enjoyable memories are the sights and sounds of our home in Glide.

I can still see Mother rolling out cinnamon rolls on the dining table and then putting them into the oven of the old wood cook stove. I remember the flatirons sitting on the back of the stove where Mother kept them hot so she could do her ironing. I'll never forget the sounds of the gas-powered Maytag washer as it chugged on the back porch and the buzz of chatter as the family gathered around the table at suppertime to a delicious portion of corn meal mush and cinnamon rolls for dessert. The leftover mush would cool overnight, and Mother would slice it in strips and fry it for breakfast with eggs and homemade bread or biscuits. I remember the soft yellow glow the kerosene lamps would make as they provided light for us in the evenings.

My earliest memory of Mother was one warm spring day when I saw her coming from the woods behind our home with her Bible in her hand. I suspect she had gone there to pray and be alone with God. I was too young to understand all of the struggles that Mother was going through at that time. She was pregnant with our younger brother and had two little kids at home. She also had six children in school that required daily care with cooking, laundry, cleaning, and a husband to look after; to add to her struggles, she was ill most of the time. Seeing her in that setting set an example for me that God and God's Word was of supreme importance.

Our world revolved around Christ and the church; I don't ever remember not going to church. Our home was a home that depended on God for all of our daily provisions. Prayer and Bible reading was an everyday event, and early on I developed a keen sense and desire for spiritual things. Some of my favorite people were the Morgans. They were preachers, and I loved to be around Mr. Morgan. He could quote entire books of the Bible by memory. I remember him preaching and saying, "We will be reading from a certain portion of the Bible." He would begin reading and never open his Bible. I kind of wanted to be like him, but I kept my thoughts to myself.

Dad was working at the veteran's hospital in Roseburg at that time. The wages were skimpy to say the least. Jim related to me how excited Dad was when he got a pay raise to $52.00 dollars a month. With this raise, Dad bought the family a giant chocolate bar and gave the children one square each. I do know that Dad was involved in a number of other ways of making a living for his family. He raised bees, cut wood with a crosscut saw, and sold Fuller brushes from door to door. Dad was open to anything that would turn a few pennies, and in those days, pennies counted a lot.

We lived off of the farm. We raised chickens for eggs and meat. Cows provided us with milk, butter, and cottage cheese, and the calves were raised for meat. Hogs were a place where we disposed of our table scraps. They also supplied us with bacon, ham, lard, soap, and other great foods. The bees gave us honey and a little cash. Every year the family would get involved with picking various fruits from the fruit orchards in the area, and Mother would can the fruit and make jams and preserves. Mother canned vegetables from the garden and berries that grew wild and plentiful in western Oregon.

Dad worked at the veteran's hospital in Roseburg about 18 miles from our home in Glide. The cost of gas was something to consider even though the price was only a few cents a gallon. Dad would have to work a whole day to buy a tankful. To help keep the cost down, he would often stay in Roseburg and sleep in the truck.

It was during this time, as Dad tells the story, that his friends encouraged him to apply for government relief. After much encouragement, Dad decided maybe he would, but he didn't want to. He said as he was walking up the steps to the courthouse, the scripture came to him: "I have been young, and now am old; yet have I not seen the righteous forsaken, nor his seed begging bread" *(Ps.36:25)*. Dad said, "I just turned around and walked back down the steps determined to trust the Lord." God did supply for us. We were never hungry or without clothing or a warm place to sleep.

I cannot say how I came to the conclusion that the family could use some help in providing for our needs, but I decided that I should do something to help. I remember that I endeavored to go into a couple of different businesses with no thought of capital or know how. The day I decided to go into the turkey business was a warm spring day.

Taking Merle, my constant companion, with me (23 months my junior), we walked to our closest neighbor, who lived about a quarter-mile to the east of our place. I knew they had turkeys, so going to their place, I knocked on the door. When Mrs. Blakely came to the door, I still remember the surprised look on her face as she looked down at two little barefoot kids, Merle dressed in a cotton dress and me in my bib overalls. Mrs. Blakely was standing there with the screen door half opened with something cradled in her arm. It looked like a mixing bowl, perhaps something she was fixing for dinner. I looked up at her and asked if she had any turkeys for sale. She said that she didn't. As we walked away heading back home, I remembered that the neighbors to the west had turkeys. They lived about a half-mile or less to the west of our place.

Merle and I walked to their place, and I knocked on the door. When the lady came to the door, I asked if she had any turkeys for sale. She said that she didn't, but she had some cookies and milk and asked if we would like some. That sounded good to me. So we went in and were enjoying our milk and cookies when a knock came to her door. She answered the door, and our father was there. He asked if we were inside, and of course we were. I never thought too much about it; however, on the way home, Dad stopped and cut a willow switch. He gave us a "lesson" on how we were not to go out on our own, even to start up a business.

With the turkey business out of the question, I thought I would butcher the chickens and sell them. I caught three or four hens, tied them up on the fence by their feet, and then went into the house to get something to kill them with. Mother wouldn't let me kill the hens. When I went out to release them, I was unable to untie the knots. I had to wait until someone else could free them. (I suppose I had seen Dad butcher chickens for market and thought I could do the same). With the idea of going into business out of the question, I settled into being a little boy and resorted to play.

One day, Merle and I were playing down by the spring. We were walking up the hill to the road that went from the highway to our house. On the uphill side of the road, Dad had placed his beehives on a plank that was sitting on a couple of apple boxes. Just as we were coming up onto the road, a honeybee stung me. That made me mad, and I said to my sister, "Come on Merle; let's beat-um-up."

At that point, I picked up a stick and proceeded to pound on the bee hives. The bees responded instantly, and soon Merle and I were on the ground screaming our lungs out.

Polly had stayed home from school that day to help Mother. When Mother and Polly heard our screams, they came running to our aid. Polly charged into the swarm of bees where we were on the ground, unable to move. The last thing I remember was her grabbing Merle and me by our hands and dragging us away from the hives.

Polly said that she and Mother were frantic and didn't know what to do. Merle and I were covered from head to toe with bee stings. Polly was also covered with bee stings. She said that the bees were in her hair, up under her dress, and on her arms and face, but she hadn't thought of her own safety. All she could think of was Merle and me. Polly later related how a few weeks before this incident, she had read that the Indians used mud to take the swelling and poison out of bee stings.

Merle, Dad & Glen
about six months after Glen decided to beat up the bees. 1940

Not stopping to think, Polly grabbed a washtub and a shovel and ran to the spring. She filled the tub with dirt pumping in water until she had a tubful of mud. She then carried the tub to the house where Mother had stripped us of our clothing. Mother and Polly then immersed us in the mud bath. I don't know how long we were in the tub of mud, but Polly said that she and Mother took 30 stingers out of Merle's forehead. It goes without saying that they were praying the whole time.

I don't remember anything about that day, from the time Polly fell the second time until Dad came home. Dad was working swing shift at the veteran's hospital in Roseburg. I remember waking up well after midnight, and Dad and Mother were standing together looking down at me.

I looked up at them and said, "Jesus healed me." I believe I would not be here today except that Jesus did heal Merle and me the day I decided to beat up the bees.

Move To Roseburg

That spring when school was out, Dad moved the family to Roseburg. We moved into a place out west of town. Melrose Road ran in front of our place with the South Umpqua River across the road. A big event occurred during the move: our little brother John William joined the family. Bill, as we called him, arrived July 21st, 1940; I don't recall having any feelings one-way or the other. Also Polly and Louie left home that summer and began to make their way in the world. Louie joined the CCC (a job conservation corps), and Polly went off to school. Polly and Lewis never returned home to live after they left that summer. Lewis joined the Navy after spending some time in the CCC camp. Polly wound up in the Los Angeles area going to a Christian college. I think we were all home for that Christmas, and then it was several years before we were all together again.

We lived at that place the school year of 1940–1941. A few things happened that might be of some interest. It was at this time that Dad started fishing a lot (at least that I remember). One day as Dad was working in the garden, he fixed me up with a string tied to a willow limb and put on a hook with a worm. Before long,

I had caught a bullhead catfish. I felt pretty special to think that I had caught my first fish.

It was at this time that I got up early one morning and asked Dad if I could go with him fishing. To my sorrow, he said no. After Dad left the house, I sat around for a while and became bored. I don't know what possessed me, but all of a sudden I ran upstairs where Sam was sleeping, and I woke him up saying that Dad said that we could go fishing with him but to put on lots of clothes 'cause it was awful cold. When he came running down the steps, I met him and said, "Ha-ha, he's already gone." Sam was not too happy about that and chased me for quite a while, but he never caught me.

As the school year came to a close that year, we moved to a small place off of Garden Valley Road. This was a little two-bedroom house that only had room enough for Mom, Dad, and the girls to have the bedrooms. We boys had our beds on the front porch. Some would say these were not very good living condition, but I thought it was great.

That summer, Grandma (Dad's mother) came to visit. I remember how excited Dad was to have her coming from Kansas. Aunt Pearl, Aunt Josie, from Kansas, and Aunt Dewy, with her daughter Rosslea, from Idaho, also came with Grandma. Lewis and Polly came from California. What a wonderful time of celebration. We had a pretty big group for such a small house, but we made it work.

The day that Louie was to arrive was a special day for me. I could hardly wait for him to get home, and when he did arrive, he looked real good in his Navy uniform. He had some real shiny black oxfords that were the prettiest shoes I had ever seen. The next day or two, Dad took me to town to buy me a new pair of shoes, and I talked him into buying me a pair of black oxfords like

Louies. I was never so proud of a pair of shoes in my whole life and Louie taught me how to tie my shoes, boy I felt special.

Dad had planned a trip to the coast while Grandma and all of the family were together. As was our custom, Dad loaded all of our belongings onto the old Chevy truck. Mother and Grandma rode up front with Dad. All the rest climbed on the back, and we went to the coast. I don't remember much about the trip, but I do recall that when we got to the coast we all ran down to the beach and began to play in the surf.

I didn't want to get my new shoes wet, so I took them off and placed them on a log and went off to play with the rest of the family. When I returned to get my shoes, I could not find them. My brothers and I hunted and hunted, but we could not find my shoes. I suppose the tide may have come in and taken my new shoes. At any rate, they were gone. My next shoes were a pair of ugly brown high tops.

With Grandma and Aunts Pearl, Jose, and Dewy returning to their respective homes, Lewis returning to the Navy, and Polly going off to school, life returned to normal. I returned to exploring the vast wilderness, hiking over the fields covered with wild rose bushes and a large heard of sheep that grazed next to our place.

Entering School

That fall, 1941, I entered the first grade, and my world began to expand. Our school was a two-room school with grades one through four in one room and grades five through eight in the other room. I think Sam and I were in the same room and Joe and Jim were in the other room. School was good. I enjoyed learning, and the new friends I made were of a great interest to me. I don't know how long we lived in the house on Garden Valley Road, but before winter, Dad found us a place at Winchester, and we moved to this new house.

The move to Winchester was a good move. The house was a large two story with enough bedrooms for us all. The one room school was just across the street, and I was in the first grade with two other boys. Shortly after we moved to Winchester, when we returned home from church Sunday evening, we received word that the Japanese had bombed Pearl Harbor. I was only six years old, but the news hit me like a thunderbolt. I didn't understand what had happened, but I knew something terrible had happened and I was plenty frightened.

Our neighborhood took on a different feeling after that day. We were not as carefree, there were blackouts, and night driving was limited; we hung blankets over our windows so no light could be seen outside. There was a neighborhood watch with everyone taking their turn to watch for any aircraft that would fly over; this was maintained around the clock. We were issued ration stamps to buy various items. I don't remember all of the things, but sugar, gas, and tires were some of the things that were rationed.

One event I learned about years later: When Mother learned about the war and having a son in the Pacific serving in the Navy, she immediately went to pray for the safety of her son. I was told that Mother prayed and fasted for over twenty days, and when asked if she had not fasted enough, her reply was, "God will tell me when it is enough." Almost five years remained in the war, and Louie was engaged in several battles, yet he never received a scratch or lost anything due to enemy conflict. God's blessing seemed to be on him as he received many commendations and advanced in rank rather quickly, finding favor with his superiors and co-workers.

As 1942 wore on, we began to relax some, and while the war was still very much in our minds, we children returned to being children. Living at Winchester was great, and I enjoyed the freedom to roam as I pleased. I hiked in the woods, played along the river, and explored the barns, and in general life was great. Sam and I would walk along the highway and pick up empty bottles and then take them to the local restaurant to sell them. We got one cent for stubby beer bottles and two cents for pop bottles. This was a great pastime and gave us a little spending money.

One day the waitress said, "If you kids don't quit bringing in all of these bottles, I am going to shoot you."

After that I didn't want to go back, but that never bothered Sam.

Learning To Ride

Dad had a calf in the pasture next to the house that he was fatting to butcher. One warm sunny day, Jim decided that I should learn to ride. That sounded okay to me. Jim and Sam caught the calf, and Sam held him while Jim tied me on so that I would not fall off and get injured. There was only one small problem: The only rope that they could find was Dad's fifty-foot anchor rope that he used when he went fishing. We knew better than to cut any of that rope, so Jim used the whole fifty feet. Jim first tied my feet together under the calf's belly. That took about two feet, so he wrapped the rest of the rope around my waist, then around the calf, then around my waist, then around the calf until he had used all of the rope. Obviously I was not going to fall off.

At this point, the calf balked and would not move, but the boys were not to be put off by a small thing like a balking calf. Jim and Sam got some sticks and poked, hit, and twisted the calf's tail until he took off on a dead run down the pasture. When the calf came to the end, he made a sharp left turn and then made another sharp left turn and headed back in the direction we had started; only he had moved over in the field to where Dad had his bee hives sitting on a plank resting on a couple of apple boxes. As the calf came by the beehives, he was too close and knocked the beehives over. All of a sudden, the bees came after the calf, and the real ride was on. All that I remember after the bees got after us is that the calf was running straight for the smoke house.

Several years later, I asked Jim, "How did I get off of the calf?"

He laughed and said that they finely cornered the calf way down in the corner of the pasture. He said that he tried to hold the calf while Sam untied me, and he added, "You know how slow Sam was." He said that calf was jumping and bucking and just about beat me to death before Sam got the rope untied. I suspect that when this was all over, the boys rolled the rope up and put it back where Dad kept it and we never thought anymore about it.

The summer of 1942 was a fun year with hiking, collecting bottles, and the calf ride. Jim went to work for a neighbor who had a big ranch up the river about a mile. I would often walk up to the ranch and visit with the Henningers. That fall when the fruit was ready to harvest, I went to work picking prunes for Mr. Henninger. I wasn't much good. My best day was only about eight boxes; however, all of the pickers were paid ten cents a box, and I made my eighty cents.

Sometimes Mr. Henninger would take me into town with him when he delivered the prunes to the packinghouse. I thought this was great fun because Mr. Henninger owned a grocery store in town. We always stopped there, and he would get me an ice cream. I always had a soft spot in my heart for the Henningers.

On several occasions, I would stay late at the Henninger's, and it would be getting dark before I got home. Walking along the river road with big fir trees overshadowing the road and the ripple of the river created a scary walk, the shadows and the evening sounds would cause me to become frightened. I discovered that if I quickened my pace, before long I would be running at full speed until I got home; however, if I could keep my fear under control, I could walk at my regular pace. That did not remove all of the fear, but I was able to control my emotions.

Move From Winchester

Before 1942 had ended, Dad made a deal with the Morgans to buy their home as they were moving to Seattle to start a new church. One night while Dad and Mother were talking with the Morgans, Sam and I happened to be with the folks. Sam and I didn't go into the house with Mom and Dad. We stayed outside, and after some time, we started to look in the icebox that was on the porch. Inside the icebox was an apple pie that had been cut into.

Well that pie looked mighty good, and anyway who would notice if a little piece was missing, so we each had a very small piece of that delicious pie. Well that tasted so good we decided to have another little tiny piece. Then we needed another little piece. Before long we had eaten the whole pie. I never heard anything about that incident, but the next time I was over to the Morgans, Mrs. Morgan presented me with a personal-size apple pie. Needless to say, I never forgot the incident or the lesson that I learned, that when you take something that you are not suppose to, a little bit will never be enough.

Before Christmas, we moved into the house Dad bought from the Morgans, and we were back in our old school district. Once again, I was going to school with my old friends. School was good, and I enjoyed learning. I don't remember school being hard for me. It seemed that I was able to grasp the lessons quickly, and I received good marks.

When school was out, I was busy exploring our new neighborhood. There were a lot of hills to hike and fields to explore. Merle and I did our share of hiking and playing in the fields.

On the 17th of May 1943, in the early afternoon, a surprise came to our home. An ambulance pulled up to our house and brought Mother home, and with her was a new baby named Chester Earl. Chester was the tenth child in our already busy family, and he was just as welcome as all of the previous children had been. I didn't know too much about babies. I never paid him much attention, and he never interfered with my world of exploring and finding new things to do.

A Spiritual Encounter

I am not sure when I first felt the draw of the Holy Spirit. I recall one Sunday when I was 6 or 7 years old, at the close of the service, the preacher gave an invitation to come to the altar and accept Jesus. I felt the desire to respond, so I went forward, kneeling at the altar and bowing my head in prayer.

No one else came forward, so the service was dismissed. People started visiting, and I was left alone at the altar. No one came to pray with me, probably thinking that I was just a kid and wasn't serious or didn't understand what I was doing. Regardless of what may or may not have been the thinking, I was embarrassed and quietly got up and slipped back into the group of people, hiding behind and out of sight as much as possible.

Our home was a home that centered on God, and prayer was a vital part of our family life. When Dad was not there to lead the family in devotions, Mother would fill in. Such was the case when I was eight years old. Dad was working in the woods logging at that time, and Mother would gather the children who were home for our devotions. While we were having our devotions, I felt the need to spend some time alone with God.

After our devotions, I went out to the barn to be alone with God and pray. Entering the barn, I went to the stanchion where the milk cow was fed. Climbing inside, I turned the feed box on edge making a place for an altar. Kneeling down at my homemade altar, I asked Jesus to come into my heart. I don't know how long I was there, probably not long, but when I left, I knew that I had received Jesus into my heart.

I went back to the house and told Mother that I had asked Jesus into my heart, and her response was, "That's nice." I then went out on the porch where my older brother and younger sister were playing and told them that I had asked Jesus into my heart. There response was laughter and jeers to which I felt ashamed and never talked about that experience again. Looking back at that time when I asked Jesus to come into my heart, I believe that He has never left me in spite of my many failures.

Moving To The Farm

Sometime before Christmas, Dad decided to go back to farming, he felt that was the best place to raise boys. By Christmas, Dad had made a trip to Redmond, Oregon and rented a farm. I was all excited to think that we were going to live on a farm. After Christmas, we loaded all of our belongs onto the old Chevrolet truck and made the move to Redmond before the New Year 1944. I loved being on the farm. There were a lot of places for me to explore. The barn was huge and offered interesting exploring, and climbing on the haystacks was great fun. We had cows, pigs, and chickens. Everything was in pens or corrals. As the old saying goes, I was in hog heaven.

Then school started, school was seven miles away in the town of Redmond, and all of us rode the bus to school. This was my first experience being on a bus. I guess that was all right, but then we got to school. That was the biggest school I had ever seen in my life. There were kids everywhere. When I found my third-grade class, I discovered it was in a building completely separate from the rest of the school. To make matters worse, there were two third-grade classrooms. Until we moved to Redmond, I had never been in a classroom without one or two of my siblings being in the same room. When we moved to Redmond, the school was such a traumatic experience that I emotionally shut down.

The whole experience was so overwhelming that I withdrew into a shell and shut down. I never entered into any class activities and would just sit in my seat. I remember the teacher making an effort to get me to open up, but I was too traumatized.

Two events occurred that I have never shared until now—may explain how withdrawn I became. One day I needed to go to the lavatory real bad, but I was afraid to ask the teacher if I could go. I held out as long as I could, and then nature took its course and I emptied my bladder. Fortunately, Dad had bought us kids some snowsuits, and the heavy snowsuit absorbed my embarrassment. The other incident occurred at lunchtime. Mother always fixed us a lunch that we carried in a brown paper bag, no big deal. However, one day when I went to get my lunch, I could not find it. Someone had taken it by mistake. When the teacher realized that I didn't have a lunch she went searching. In a few moments, she returned with a nice lunch, but it wasn't mine and I refused to eat it.

Back To Roseburg

Dad's health wasn't doing too well with the climate there at Redmond, so within a few months, we moved back to Roseburg. By the time we made the move, I had become so traumatized and had shut down so completely that I had lost all of the educational gains I had made in the first two and a half years of school.

In the spring of 1944, we moved into a large house on Walnut Street in the north part of Roseburg. This was to be the last home I lived in until I joined the Air Force in October 1952. I thought that house was a great place to live. We had one electric light in the dining room and cold water piped into the kitchen that was heated by coils running through the firebox of the wood cook stove. Saturday baths were taken in a wash tub, and we had a two-holer and a path, properly known as an outhouse, but it was home and I loved it.

Going to school was quite an experience. This was a new school to me, and there were two third-grade rooms. I was so far behind the rest of the class that it was impossible for me to catch up. By this time, I was convinced that I was unable to learn, and my new third grade teacher wasted no time in confirming what I thought. When she finished with me, there was no doubt that I was stupid and learning was beyond my ability. As school came to a close that year and the report cards were given out, my card read, "Glen Suiter remains in the third grade." As the students walked out of the school sharing their report cards and all being promoted to the next grade, I shared my card. I laughed outside, but inside, I was devastated; however, this was more confirmation of how dumb I was, and I felt that I deserved to fail. This also added to the feeling that I was unacceptable.

With school out, I turned my attention to exploring my new neighborhood. There were hills to hike, creeks to play in, fields to roam over, and I could do mostly what I wanted. Dad would take me fishing from time to time, and I liked to go with him. Sometimes we would walk down to the river that was only about ¾ mile from our home.

One day I was rummaging around in the hall closet at the bottom of the stairs. There I found a pair of Dad's rubber knee boots. I had my shoes on and slipped my feet into Dad's boots. With my shoes on, the boots seemed to fit. I walked around the front yard for a while feeling rather important. Then a thought hit me: These would make great hip boots for me.

I decided to go fishing, so I got the fishing pole down and found some worms by looking under some boards lying around on the ground. Then I headed for the river wearing my new hip boots, carrying the fishing pole and worms. I don't know how long I fished, but I soon tired and decided to return home. The trip home was not the same as the trip to the river. I was tired, and the boots were heavy and clumsy. The fishing pole was difficult to carry, and the worms were discarded. The longer I walked, the heaver those boots became. Soon I was wishing that I never had those boots on, but I had to get home and I had to get there with those boots.

I did make it home, and I was able to take those boots off and putting them back in the closet was a great relief. I never thought too much about that incident after that, but as I look back over my life, I think that I followed that pattern a lot. I tended to jump into things before I was ready, and wearing Dad's boots before I grew into them would bring a lot of stress into my life.

When school started that fall, I returned to the third grade with a new teacher. I guess I did all right. I really don't remember too much about that year as far as school is concerned. When school was out, I was passed onto the fourth grade.

That summer, Dad was logging with a partner taking piling from his farm. Dad had us boys helping in the woods; we were peeling the bark off of the logs. I was privileged to go to work with the older boys and Dad. I loved being out in the woods. One day I cut my leg with an ax while I was cutting the limbs from the log, before peeling the bark. I was never so proud of an injury in my life.

Later that summer, Mother wanted to visit her folks, so Dad sent her back to Kansas and the mid-west for a visit. We took the 1937 Ford sedan with Joe and Jim as drivers, and the four younger kids and Mother made a full carload. I haven't a clue how long we drove, but before we returned to Oregon, I met and saw relatives I didn't know existed. I met my Grandmother, Dad's mother. I hadn't seen her since 1941, and I didn't remember anything about her. I met Mother's parents for the first time. Grandpa and Grandma Fry were old and lived in a small house in Liberal, MO. I remember Grandpa was glad to see us, and I liked him. We also met other relatives. I was surprised to find we had so many. All that I had ever known were brothers and sisters.

Shortly after we returned home, World War II ended with the bombing of Japan. I remember the big celebrations and that everyone was shouting for joy. We knew that Lewis would be coming home soon, and life looked good.

That fall, I entered the fourth grade. I liked my teacher and thought that I was doing fine. As school progressed, I don't remember too much about the lessons. It seems like a blur to me. However, at the close of the year when the report cards were given out, I looked at my card, and it read, "Glen Suiter remains in the fourth grade." This time I was surprised because I thought I was doing okay. This really set me back mentally and seemed to take away all of the confidence that I had left. I was ashamed to be around other kids because I had failed twice. Nothing was ever said at home one way or the other, but I knew that I had to be the dumbest kid in the world.

From the time I failed the fourth grade, school never held much attraction for me. I went to class but never studied or applied myself to learn. My feeling was, "What was the use? I couldn't learn anyway." As a result I withdrew into a shell of survival, just getting by and not making waves, keeping a low profile so as not to create more problems for myself. I very seldom asked for anything, and if I could not get it on my own, I did without.

The Teen Years

Entering puberty brings its own set of struggles. I don't remember anything special that was earth shaking, just the normal struggles that teens face. I had very little interaction at home, I was pretty much on my own and did what I felt like doing. Learning life's lessons and interacting with others was a challenge because of my lack of confidence. There were times when life was fun, and yet life was filled with many complexities. School was not much of a problem because by this time I had given up on learning, believing I was too dumb to learn anyway. My years in grammar school had solidified that in my mind. My self esteem and self confidence were completely destroyed by this time. The only thing I could hold onto for some kind of security was my faith in God. And that was very shaky since I had no concept of faith.

My teen years were to me not eventful. I did pretty much what I wanted when I wanted. I had family chores to do. My chores consisted of milking the cow morning and night, gathering in the wood for the stove, and hoeing the garden in the summer. Sometimes I was asked to help out with other duties, but most of my time was my own. I was usually busy finding a job and working.

Family 1950:
Back row, Glen, Lewis (Louie), Dad, Mother, Joe, Opal, Merle.
Front row, John (Bill), Jim, Pauline (Polly), Sam, Chester

I used to mow lawns with one of my friends who lived in town. I would walk to his place about 2 miles away, then we would take their push lawn mower and walk around town knocking on doors when we saw a lawn that needed to be cut. We would mow the lawn and trim it with hand clippers for 25 to 75 cents depending on the size. I was always looking for something that would make me a few dollars. I picked beans, had a paper route, stacked wood, cleaned bricks, and picked berries and sold them. One summer, I and another friend (Ronnie Owen, Jim's brother in-law) would hitchhike out to the country club and caddy for the golfers. This was for tips. I did fairly well at this, but the work was hard. Most of the golfers had shoulder bags, and they were pretty heavy.

When I was 15, I went to the coast to work for a man spraying weeds along the highway. One of our neighbor boys knew the man, and his folks had a cabin we could stay in. This all sounded good to me, and I was excited about being on my own and working. The problem was I was quite small and the man thought I wasn't strong enough to do the work. I stayed there for about three weeks trying to get on with the crew only to be rejected.

During this time, on Wednesday evening the community church across the street from the cabin where we were staying was having youth services. I made up my mind to attend, and I enjoyed the service. When I came out of the church, the fellows I would have been working with on the spray crew began to tease me about going to church. To my surprise I didn't care and was glad I had gone to church. When it became evident that I was not going to get the job, I packed my suitcase and hitchhiked back home.

Living a spiritual life was very difficult because I was never able to measure up to what a Christian was suppose to be. By this time, I had started smoking and going places that were strictly against the church rules. The rules were simple enough: no picture shows, no dancing, no pool halls, no skating rinks, no alcohol, no smoking, no hunting on Sunday, no fishing on Sunday—I am sure I have forgotten a few things. For a person to be a Christian, these were the things we were expected to follow, and if you didn't, you were considered a backslider and were on your way to hell, no ifs, ands, or buts about it. The girls had it worse than the boys because they had dress codes added to their restrictions.

I lived my life based totally on how I felt. If I felt saved, I acted like a Christian; if I felt unsaved, I acted unsaved. I don't ever remember being told faith in God had nothing to do with feelings. I don't ever remember being taught the security of trusting in God for salvation as a matter of faith. I would be remiss if I said the church didn't teach faith as a basis for salvation, for they did; but somehow as a teen I never caught the concept of living by faith.

My faith and I had a real hard time during my teen years. It seemed like I could never live up to the standard that people or I thought that I should. The church that we attended had some strict guidelines that they believed if not followed you were a backslidden Christian and were on your way to hell. This was either stated or implied, at least I took it to heart living on a roller coaster of spiritual emotion.

The church would have revival meetings at least twice a year, and the teens would go to the altar and give our heart to God. We would pray and commit our lives to serve the Lord for the rest of our lives. I can't speak for the rest of the teens, but I was dead serious every time I made that commitment. By the time Wednesday would roll around, I no longer felt saved. I was depending completely on my feelings for my salvation.

Because I no longer had the feelings that I had the first couple of days. I would give up trying to be a Christian. I would then revert to doing what I felt like, namely living as a backslider. Determined to not be a hypocrite, I would declare that I was not a Christian and returned to my old sinful ways. This would mean going with the crowd and doing whatever my friends suggested. The sad thing is that I didn't have any faith to stand on. I didn't know that once you were born into the family of God it wasn't that easy to fall away.

It is not my intent to be critical of our church and their teaching. I believe the church was trying to keep their people from sin and to present them to God as a holy people. I am grateful for my church and the standards they set even though I was unable to live up to them. I was always aware of where I was in my Christian walk, and while I failed many times, I still had a line that I would not cross.

My inability to maintain my Christian commitment caused me to treat God and the church the same way I treated school. I withdrew from both—God and the church. I didn't like myself or the path I was walking. It seemed that I was mostly tolerated by my friends and the adults of the church. I fully accepted this place in life because of failing the third and fourth grades. I knew I didn't deserve any better.

I didn't believe that God could like me because I was so dumb. It is interesting to note that many times during this period when I was alone I would find a place and have some private time with God, although I was always disappointed because I never had the feeling that God listened to me.

I have since learned that faith in God has nothing to do with feelings. It is totally dependent upon God's word and what he said he would do. After that day when I went to the barn and ask Jesus into my heart and life, I am convinced that God has never left me in spite of how I felt.

My social life was quite limited. I had two friends that I would call close friends. Fred was a school friend. We were about the same age. I spent a lot of time with him. His dad was a logger. He would take Fred and me with him to the woods from time to time. I always liked going to the woods. I loved the outdoors. Fred and I liked to go camping. We would take food and bedding, and after making our camp, we would spend the rest of the time running over the hills or up and down the river bank depending on where we were camping. Fred's mother would take us to our camp and pick us up at the prescribed time.

One day after school, there was a big fire on the hill east of our home. Fred and I decided to go up and see the fire first hand.

We took Fred's bike and headed out to see the fire. We were riding double—my bike was most likely broke down. I would sit on the crossbar of his bike. This was a common way to ride double at that time. We were unable to ride the bike up the hill, so we pushed it up the hill, which happened to be a long dirt road and quite steep. When we were almost to the top of the hill, there was a little incline down before the last climb up to the top where we could see the fire. We decided to ride down as far as we could before the last climb. Getting on the bike, I was on the crossbar and Fred on the seat and peddling; we started down the incline. We hadn't gone very far when I caught the heel of my shoe in the spokes of the front wheel and ripped out all but a few of the spokes. There we were up on the hill a couple of miles from home with a disabled bike.

There was nothing left to do but try to get that bike back home. We tried to carry the disabled bike, but that proved to be more than we were willing to do. Fred had a great idea, so we left the bike on the hillside and walked home. When we got home and told our story to his mother, she put us in her car and drove us to where we had left the bike. We loaded the bike into the trunk of their car and got it home the easy way.

My other friend was older than me and went to the same church. Alfred was tall and slim with dark hair. I liked being with him because it made me feel good to be with an older person giving me a feeling of acceptance. For about three years, Al and I were always together doing things and going places. Al influenced me into a life that I didn't like much, but I liked being with him. We would stay out late at night and roam the streets. I started to smoke and go to shows, the pool halls, and other questionable places—things that were strictly against the rules of the church. By this time I had gained the reputation of being a bad boy.

Entering High School

Graduating from the eighth grade was no big deal to me. There were no acknowledgements one way or the other. That summer I got my driver's license and acquired a car, a 1936 Chevy sedan. That gave me some feeling of independence.

As it came time for school to start, I went to the high school and registered with all of the other freshmen. I received my assignments and started school. I was somewhat taken aback by the different classes. They were not that much different from junior high, but they were more challenging.

Three weeks after I entered the ninth grade, in the fall of 1951, I was at a small grocery store with other students on our lunch break when Al drove up driving a shiny yellow Chevy convertible. Al had just returned from a trip he had taken to southern California to visit his brother. Al talked me into cutting class and going for a drive. That cut started a trend that continued for the rest of the year. I would cut school as much as two weeks at a time.

At first I would miss one day and then two. Soon I was missing a whole week. I really never thought too much about it. I was not aware of any concern from my father or mother as nothing was ever said. Shortly after I started cutting school, Al and I went to work for a building contractor cleaning up around the building site and digging ditches for drain fields, before backhoes came into being.

Typically after I had missed more than a week of school, I would come home to find my father and the truant officer waiting for me. He and Dad would talk to me about returning to school; I would always agree to, but would only stay one or two days and then be gone again. The scenario continued until spring when a change of events allowed me to completely leave school.

In the spring of 1952, Dad wanted to move to the coast and spend his retirement years fishing; he bought a 30 foot commercial fishing boat and some property on the coast. Dad wanted me to go to the coast with him, and this gave me the opportunity I was looking for to quit school. I wrote a note to the school stating that Glen was moving to Coos Bay and would not be returning to school for the rest of the year. I then signed it J. W. Suiter, when I took the note into the school office, the school discharged me and I never heard any more about school. I was 16 at that time.

With school out of the way, I was able to enjoy the new freedom that I had. I did go to the coast with Dad and helped him build a little house where Mother and the three younger children lived through the summer. I fished with Dad all that summer. I liked being with Dad. It was the only time in my life that I had much of a relationship with him. I didn't care much for being out on the water. The days were long and kind of boring, however I liked being with Dad. We talked a lot, but not about life—mostly small talk. We talked about navigation, the sea, fishing, the weather, and things like that. Quite often, we would go out in the fog and have to follow the compass to the fishing grounds and follow the compass home at night. I got to where I could navigate pretty well. I thought that I might like to be a navigator, but then I knew I was too dumb for that so quickly dropped that idea.

The year I turned seventeen, I spent the summer fishing with Dad and for the most part enjoyed my time with him. That summer I attended church with the family. I really enjoyed church and even joined the choir. At the close of the season, I returned to Roseburg and my old friends, but things were not the same as before. I was not comfortable being around them, and I began looking for a way out of the life I had been living.

That year, when deer season opened, Joe invited me to go hunting with him and his father-in-law in eastern Oregon. I jumped at the chance, and for the next week we camped and hunted. I loved being out in the woods by myself. We never hunted on Sundays, so late that Sunday afternoon I took the rifle and walked down a dirt road beside a hay field. As I was walking, I began to think about what I wanted to do with my life. I suppose many thoughts came to my mind, but they soon lost importance to me for all of a sudden the thought came, "I want to be a preacher." I had no idea how that would ever come about, but there was no doubt that was what I was going to give my life to. At this time I was not claiming to be a Christian. I was still smoking, and you couldn't be a Christian and smoke. I didn't know when but I knew that someday I would make the commitment and I would be strong enough to stand and be a minister.

I never shared this experience with anyone because I was afraid they would laugh at me. I also remembered how, when we were younger, teens would stand after a special meeting and say how they were going to be preachers and missionaries. Then they would soon forget that calling, and I didn't want to be like them. This was a very special moment for me, and I wanted to treat it as a special time between God and me. I knew God had placed his hand on me for service when I was eight, and He confirmed it as I walked down that dusty road beside the hay field.

When we returned home from our hunt, without any deer, I was left to wonder some more. Life seemed empty, and I didn't know what to do with myself since school was not an option. My brother Sam had just been home on leave from the Air Force and had been shipped out to England.

Within a few weeks after our hunting trip, I was walking down the street when I saw an Air Force recruiter. All of a sudden, I decided to join the Air Force. I had turned seventeen that August, and I was old enough to join with my parent's permission. I went into his office and got the necessary papers and took them home and showed them to Mother and Dad. They agreed to sign for me, and within a week I was on my way to Portland to join the Air Force. I rode to Portland with my older brother Joe. He told me to keep a good attitude and never complain about the duty: "Just do your job and you will be okay." I took his advice and spent the next four years in the Air Force.

My Time In The Air Force

October 28, 1952, I was inducted into the Air Force. I weighed 113 pounds and stood 5 ft. 6 in. and had a 28 inch waist. I was underweight, but they thought I would gain the necessary two more pounds soon enough. There were three other fellows that joined with me. We flew from Portland to Oakland, California. From there we were bussed out to Parks Air Force Base, near Oakland, CA. where I went through basic training.

A chance meeting changed my entire life. When I went to Portland to join the Air Force, I happened to meet a man from Myrtle Creek, OR. who was inducted one day ahead of me. We talked some while waiting to ship out to basic training. I never thought too much about him although I liked him, and it was nice to know someone from close to my home town. We never had any contact during basic, but at the conclusion of basic, we both were shipped to Sheppard A.F.B. for aircraft mechanical training.

While at Sheppard, we were in the same barracks. It was there that I learned that Jack was a Christian. I went with him to Youth for Christ meetings. I enjoyed being with him, but in my mind, I was a backslider and wasn't living a Christian life, so our time was limited. Jack attended the Assembly of God Church, and I was Nazarene.

At the conclusion of training, Jack and I were both shipped to Moses Lake, Washington. We had the same time to report and were in the same wing, though different squadrons. Jack and I agreed to travel together from our home to Moses Lake in his car. Arriving in Moses Lake, we didn't know anyone else yet so we became buddies.

On Sunday, Jack said, "Let's go to church." That sounded good to me, but I had no idea where we would go. Jack suggested that we attend the Assembly of God church in Ephrata, a neighboring town to the air base.

We found that the church was meeting in the Seventh Day Adventist building because they didn't have a place of their own. During the service, we learned they were in the process of building a church and that it was the pastor's last Sunday. After the service, the pastor ask Jack and I if we wanted to work. We said yes, thinking he wanted us to help with the new church building. He told us to be at his home the next evening when we got off work at the base. We agreed to be there.

To our surprise, the pastor, Clayton Nash, didn't want us to help on the church. He had a janitorial business and wanted us to do janitorial work in town. We went to work and continued to work as long as we were in Moses Lake. It is interesting how little events have a way of becoming major turning points in a person's life. I learned that Jack's uncle was the pastor of the Assembly of God Church in Myrtle Creek, Oregon. Jack was a strong, committed Christian, and I liked that about him. We attended church regularly and encouraged other service men to join us.

Glen: Air Force 1955

I still was not professing to be a Christian, believing myself to be a backslider. As time passed, I became very involved with the Nashes going with them to visit their relatives and attending different churches with them. The Nashes, Clayton and Betty, took us in as one of their own and treated us like family. I grew close to the Nash family and enjoyed being with them as much as possible.

We had worked for Clayton for about 10 months when Jack received word that his uncle had resigned the church in Myrtle Creek and was leaving. Jack was quite upset, so to encourage Jack, Clayton said, "Don't worry, Jack, I will go down and be the pastor." I don't know if that made Jack feel any better or not, but Clayton did become the pastor of the church.

The time I spent in Moses Lake, I attended the Assembly of God church in Ephrata. I liked the new pastor and enjoyed the services. While there I learned a little chorus that has stayed with me, and I refer to it quite often.

The story that the pastor related to us happened while he was in the Navy during World War II. They were in the South Pacific on an aircraft carrier. When the planes returned from a mission, one of the planes was too badly damaged to land on the ship. The pilot, realizing he was unable to land, turned his plane out toward the sea away from the ship. The last words that were heard from the pilot was him singing this chorus:

Got any rivers you think are uncross able.
Got any mountains you can't tunnel through.
God specializes in things thought impossible, and
He will do what no other power can do.

That summer, the unit we were assigned to was transferred to Donaldson Air Force Base at Greenville, South Carolina. Jack had recently married and didn't want to move, so he applied for a transfer to stay in Moses Lake. His request was granted, and I went with the unit to South Carolina. We remained friends and connected from time to time over the next several years, even after we separated from the service.

I arrived at Donaldson AFB in the summer of 1954. Shortly after settling in, I applied to become a flight mechanic. I was accepted, and for the next two years I traveled with the airplane I was assigned to. I seemed to be on the move all of the time. We flew short hops and long distance. The job was to fly with the plane and perform the mechanical duties. Part of the job was to keep a watch on all areas of the plane in flight and climb out through the wings and check the engines while in flight. I thought this was a great job and was able to travel to many parts of the world: mostly Europe, North Africa, South America, the U.S., and north into the arctic. What an opportunity to see different places. Although we never saw much of the country, at least I could say I had been there.

While in Rome, I had quite an experience. I was traveling with about 20 other airman. I don't recall the nature of the mission. However, we were in Rome for a few days. While there, a friend and I took a horse drawn buggy tour of the city. We saw several sights, but the ones I remember were the coliseum and the dungeon where Saint Paul was imprisoned. I was impressed with the history of the city. My only regret was that I could not speak Italian and our guide could not speak English.

My time in the service was sprinkled with times of spiritual encounters, but for the most part, I lived a life of sin. I still smoked, drank alcohol, and went with the boys; however, there was still a line I would not cross. I was very careful to never do anything that would hinder me from my desire of becoming a preacher.

There were times when I went to church and encouraged my friends to join me. I was never bashful about that. I listened to gospel programs and even prayed from time to time. But the "feeling" was never there, so I would give up and go on doing what I was doing, knowing that someday I would hit pay dirt and my life would be changed.

The fall before I separated from the Air Force, I took a 30 day leave. While home, I went hunting with my Dad, brother, and three friends. After arriving at our hunting place, which we were not familiar with, we separated, each going in a different direction. I went up the hill and along a ridge watching the hillside as I walked. I was paying attention to where I was and the direction I was going. There was three or four inches of snow on the ground, which made for easy walking. As I walked, the fog moved in, and I lost my landmarks.

As the day progressed, without seeing any deer, I decided to return to the car. I went down the hill to the road where I thought the car was parked. Walking up the road, I soon discovered I was on the wrong road. So I retraced my steps, climbing back up the hill to where I had started. At the top, I again headed in the direction of the car. To my surprise, I found I had circled and come back to where I started seeing my tracks in the snow. Realizing what had happened, I became aware that I was lost, and had no idea which direction to go.

At that point, I stopped and thought about my situation. I did not panic. I remembered my training and thought, "SOS, a distress signal." I fired three rounds spaced to indicate a distress. Right away I heard the sound of the car horn. Instantly I knew where I was and what direction to go to reach the car.

As I have reflected on that event, I found it to be a great life lesson. Many times we find ourselves in a situation where we are lost and unsure as to which way to go. That is the time not to panic but to stop and send out a distress signal to our Heavenly Father and wait for the answer. When we receive the answer, we can move ahead with full confidence.

As the time for my discharge drew near, my thoughts were more and more on what I was going to do. Someone suggested that I reenlist. That was not for me. It was time for me to give myself wholly to God and prepare for the ministry. I shared my thought with only a couple of my friends and received some encouragement to follow my dream.

After my separation from the service, I had only one goal, and that was to make that final commitment. This did not come as easily as I hoped. It seemed that I could not find God anywhere.

On my way home, I stopped to visit my aunt in Kansas. While there, I went to church and went to the altar and tried to change, but by noon the next day, I was back where I started. I came home and went to church with my folks, but I didn't feel welcome by the church—too much old history.

When Jack encouraged me to attend the church in Ephrata, that started a relationship with the Nash family that lasted for years to come. When I separated from the service, Clayton and Betty were still the pastors of the Myrtle Creek Assembly of God Church. I would go down often to visit, and Clayton would come to Roseburg to visit me. He would invite me to church, and I went a few times. Basically he made me feel welcome at his home and in the church.

One day, Clayton was in Roseburg, and we had lunch. After lunch, as he dropped me off at work, he invited me to come down to church. I responded with a question: "Do you have any girls?" He said yes. That settled it. I was there for church. After a couple of months, I went to a Wednesday evening service, and when the invitation was given I responded and did hit pay dirt. God met me that night, and my life has never been the same since. I went home, took my cigarettes, and tossed them out of my room and never picked them up from that time. I was determined to live for Jesus and be the best Christian I could be. I knew that I was now ready to pursue my desire to be a minister. I did not know how or when, but I knew it would happen someday.

I don't think Jack ever knew the impact that he had in the outcome of my life. Only God knows that what seems to be a casual meeting will turn out to be life changing.

Marriage

I continued to attend the church of my friend and picked out the best-looking girl in the church to date. Our relationship blossomed, and we had a lot of fun together. We would often be laughing or giggling over one thing or another, and I was taken by her beauty. I thought her parents were the most spiritual people that I had ever known. They were the first into the prayer room, a room in the back of the church set aside for prayer, and I loved being in the prayer room with them. After we dated for several months, I asked Virginia to be my wife. She was somewhat reluctant, but after a while agreed to my request. The date was set, and her folks were delighted and welcomed me into their family.

During this time, I was growing in my young spiritual walk with God, and His word was beginning to speak to me and give me strength in my daily walk. I still struggled with the desire to smoke and thoughts that kept coming into my mind. I was told by my oldest sister that you can't stop the birds from flying in the air, but you can stop them from lodging in the branches—meaning you can't stop the thoughts from coming, but you don't have to dwell on them. The scripture was also speaking to me, and a song was always a big help.

I was reading the Scripture daily, and a couple of passages really spoke to me during my times of temptation:

> *Galatians 6:7 Be not deceived; God is not mocked: for whatsoever a man soweth, that shall he also reap. 8 For he that soweth to his flesh shall of the flesh reap corruption; but he that soweth to the Spirit shall of the Spirit reap life everlasting.*

I took to heart what the Bible said and determined to be careful of what kind of seed I was sowing, what kind of attitude I had, and what my motive was—was it to honor God or myself?

Another Scripture that helped when temptation would be almost overwhelming was 1 Corinthians 10:13:

> *There hath no temptation taken you but such as is common to man: but God is faithful, who will not suffer you to be tempted above that ye are able; but will with the temptation also make a way to escape, that ye may be able to bear it.*

The thought that all temptations were common to men meant that I was not the only one that was faced with this temptation. I therefore was not to feel defeated because of the temptation. And God promises that He will provide a way of escape. I did not have to fear being tripped up by any temptation.

Oh, How I Love Jesus—this little chorus was a constant companion when the desire to smoke was strongest and when other temptations came. I sang this chorus many times a day, every day for several years and still sing it when my mind is plagued with difficult thoughts that trouble me.

I learned that little chorus, from an old retired minister in our church, when I was a teenager. I don't recall his name, but he would always stand and testify, and he always concluded by saying, "It ain't none of the Devils business," and then sing the song:

> *Oh, how I love Jesus. Oh, how I love Jesus. Oh, how I love Jesus because he first loved me.*

That simple little song has seen me through some troubling times and given me an anchor in the midst of many a storm.

I learned early on to trust the Bible for all of my questions and not to trust in what people said the Bible said. My Dad encouraged me not to trust in man but to trust in the Word of God, and after a few times of listening to some preacher and quoting him to Dad, Dad would say that is not what the Bible says and would tell me what the Bible actually said. I learned to find out for myself what the Bible said before quoting or giving an answer to someone.

Dad explained to me that I should never trust in a human being or man to follow as examples. Dad said, "While there are good men, man will fail you; always put your trust in Jesus. He will never fail you." I have followed that advice all of my adult life and found it to be true. Some of the people I had the most trust in have stumbled, and some have downright been a disappointment. All in all, by following the advice to always keep my eyes on Jesus, it doesn't matter what others do. My faith does not rest in them; it rests in Jesus. And the Bible says that He is the same yesterday today and forever *(Heb.13:8)*. The spring and summer before our marriage was the most carefree time of my life. I was happy working in the local church teaching a Sunday school class and being given the opportunity to preach my first sermon. It didn't go well, but I was happy to try. Prayer and Bible reading seemed to occupy my time when I wasn't with Virginia. I felt good and knew I was on track to fulfill my desire to be a preacher. Our wedding was in August. I felt like I was in heaven on earth; things couldn't have been better.

Glen & Virginia's wedding picture,
with our parents Mom & Dad Suiter, Mom & Dad Cambron, 1957

Eagle Point

About a month after our wedding, Virginia's parents took a church in southern Oregon and asked us to join them. The church had been closed because the former pastor was killed in a plane crash. The church was in the process of building a new building, but everything had stopped with the death of the pastor. The church was in a very rundown condition and needed a lot of work to just get it ready to hold services. After much prayer and testing the Lord, I felt it was right for us to join them in their ministry. By October, we were living in Eagle Point, OR, and I was working full-time on the church grounds and building.

I served as youth minister and Sunday school teacher and led the worship service. I was often asked to preach for different churches when their pastor was away. I loved the chance to preach and took every opportunity presented to me. Money was tight as I never received a salary for working on the church. I never thought about the lack as I threw all of my energy and time into building and never thought about needing a job. Occasionally I worked a day or two for a logging company, but that was few and far between. It seemed the only thing I was concerned about was building the church and serving God to the best of my ability.

On one occasion, I remember sitting on the sofa having a pity party. I don't remember what for, but I was enjoying it to the fullest when God seemed to step in and gave me a song. I was not happy about that since I was having such a good time feeling sorry for myself. The song was "The Love of God."

O love of God, how rich and pure!
How measureless and strong!
It shall forevermore endure,
The saints' and angels' song.

Could we with ink the ocean fill,
And were the skies of parchment made;
Where every stalk on earth a quill,
And every man a scribe by trade;
To write the love of God above
would drain the ocean dry;
Nor could a scroll contain the whole,
Though stretched from sky to sky.

The chorus and the third verse really spoke to me. How could I feel sorry for myself and think of the words of this song? Needless to say, I got over my pity party and went back to work on the church. That song has become a mainstay in my life. When I feel down or discouraged I go back to The Love of God.

There were many blessings as Virginia and I poured our lives into the work in Eagle Point. One of the greatest blessings was July 1, 1958: our son David joined our family. The church was completed, and we were worshiping in the new sanctuary. The congregation was growing, and I was free to look for work. At this time, I took a job at a lumber mill. The work was hard, but I enjoyed working there. I also was receiving more calls to fill in for different churches in the area. It was at this time I began thinking of going to Bible College to better prepare for ministry.

Some of the older pastors told me not to go to college because I would come out losing my Spirituality and be a carbon copy, preaching what I was taught and not what God wanted. I liked what they said because I didn't have a high school education, and I really did depend on God for my messages, some of which were good for a novice.

Applying For College

I couldn't get away from the fact that I needed a better education. In August, I applied to Northwest College of the Assemblies of God and was accepted. That fall I quit my job, loaded up my family, and made the move to Seattle. Entering college was a huge challenge for me since I had no high schooling at all, but God was with me and I survived the first year. I loved the Bible classes and school in general. All in all, I managed to get a passing grade. I must say that I learned a lot about the educational system and enjoyed all of my classmates.

Money was tight, and work was inconsistent, although I did have VA benefits that kept us from going in the hole. God was faithful to supply all our needs. On one occasion, I came in late on Friday night from a mission service. Virginia greeted me and said that we didn't have any milk for the baby.

My response to her was, "God has never failed us and He will supply." The next morning I started a new job, and at our second delivery, the lady gave each of us a dollar tip. We were delivering pianos and organs. I took the dollar home and went to the store and bought a quart of milk, a pound of hamburger, and a head of lettuce. We had milk for the baby and dinner for us. God did supply.

Chasing The Ministry

When school was out, we went back to Oregon to work for the summer. The presbyter over the churches in Southern Oregon asked me if I would be open to pastoring a small church in that area. I prayed about it and thought it would be a good idea especially since my grades at school were, I thought, very poor. I thought I could do this, and it gave me a grown up feeling. I remember Dr. Butterfield, the college president, preaching a message in chapel one day. The subject was about a battle that Israel was engaged in, and the captain of the battle needed to send a message back to the king. The captain dispatched a runner to take the message, and off he went with the message. There was a young man standing there, and he wanted to run. The captain told him that he didn't have the message, but the young man insisted that he wanted to run, so the captain told him to go ahead and run. The passage of Scripture is found in 2 Samuel 18:19-32.

The young runner caught up with the old runner and passed him. When the watchman on the wall of the city saw a man running the king said, "It is a message from the battle. Let him in."

When the young runner came before the king the king questioned how goes the battle? The young runner replied, "I don't know."

At that time, the old runner was seen coming in, and he had the message. Application: Don't go into ministry until you are ready and have a message. Needless to say I thought I could run unprepared, but I found I couldn't. Wearing Dad's boots again.

While Virginia and I were pastoring at Shady Cove, Oregon, during a Sunday evening service, a group of boys kicked the front door, and then, opening the door, shouted some obscenities and left. This broke the spirit of the church, and the people began to weep. God spoke to me and said, "Have a Jericho march." Let me explain my feelings about Jericho marches, and the conditions we were living under, and about the use of spiritual gifts.

When we took the church, there was no congregation, no money, and we didn't have any place to go but up, and up was not in numbers. There were times we felt the presence of the Devil so strongly that we were afraid to look out the window because we knew we would see him looking in. At times we would hear people running in the church. The house was next to the church. On investigation, I would find the church closed and no one there, only a very ominous fearful feeling that something was not right. This unholy presence was there to the point that we just learned to live with it.

As to my feeling about a Jericho march, a Jericho march was designed after the Biblical account of Joshua's march around the walls of Jericho where the walls came tumbling down. I had never heard of such a thing until I joined the Pentecostal church. On different occasions someone would feel the spirit move them, and they would jump up and start a Jericho march, and all the church would join in. They would march around the inside of the church singing and clapping their hands. I felt this was unnecessary but would go with the flow, although I never really got into it.

My thoughts concerning the gifts of the spirit: Growing up in the Church of the Nazarene, the gifts were never mentioned. I was taught that speaking in tongues was of the devil and something to be avoided. So for me to become a part of the Pentecostal movement was quite a leap. The Bible talks about the gifts in a positive way and even something to be desired. The Bible also says to judge when the gifts are being used to see if they are of God. After being in the church for a time, I began to listen when someone would exercise the gift of tongues and try to interpret what they were saying. I discovered that most of the time the same people were exercising the gift and the messages were basically the same with some slight variations. I fully believed in the gifts, but I felt the gifts really didn't add that much to the service. This is just me and the way I looked at things at that time.

Now back to my story. When God said, "Have a Jericho march," I thought that would be okay, so I told the congregation what we were going to do. We probably had eight or ten in our group, and I was not bothered by them. As we began our march, we were singing When We All Get to Heaven. As I reached the entry door, God said, "Go outside and around the parking lot." I said nothing but continued my way around the inside of the church. God left me at the entrance door, and I walked the rest of the way by myself.

When I got back to the platform, a lady in the church, who always was giving a message in tongues, began to speak in tongues and gave a message. This lady would always give a message in tongues but would never interpret the message. For some reason God gave me the interpretation, and it was not pretty. God said, "Your heart is full of pride. You have disobeyed me and I cannot work unless you obey me." I knew where that rebuke was coming from. I told the congregation that God had told me to go outside and around the parking lot, but I had disobeyed. Their response was, "We will go," and I said, "You are not the one I was worried about. It was me."

We started the Jericho march again, but this time when we reached the entry door, we went outside singing, "When We All Get to Heaven." We marched down the front steps of the church, around the parking lot, and then back up the steps into the church. God made me walk the whole way by myself, I mean without any assurance that God was with me. When we stepped back into the church, it seemed like heaven had come down, and we had a real time of worship and praise.

From that night until the day we resigned from the church, we never had any encounter with the devil looking into our windows. No more running in the church in the middle of the night. No more problems with the kids of the community. God brought complete victory and deliverance to us and put a hedge of protection around us. The day we resigned, the oppression came back. That is when we realized what God had done for us.

Lessons learned: Sometimes God uses unorthodox methods to accomplish His will. I have never had another Jericho march. I have never given another interpretation to a message in tongues. I am sure that pride has been in my life from time to time, but I have endeavored to not let it keep me from following what I believed God asked me to do. I learned that obedience will always bring God's victory.

I have seen God work in some unusual ways, but I have not seen Him work the same way twice. I have been in services where people tried to emulate what worked once to achieve the same results. That does not work. I believe God chooses to not follow the same pattern so as to keep people trusting in Him and not in the process.

We stayed there for about two years, but all we were able to do was keep the doors open. Our average attendance was about ten to thirteen. I did get some experience at preparing sermons and preaching, but I was lacking in so many other ways.

While at Shady Cove, Gwendolyn joined the family on January 20, 1960. And then in January 1961, Kenneth was born on the 25th day. Needless to say, this put a huge strain on Virginia physically and emotionally. I was so caught up in my own struggles that I was oblivious of her needs. We resigned the church in February and moved into Medford. There I went to work at a local shoe store selling shoes.

I felt like things were going well. We had a nice home, I had a job, and we were settling in with our three little ones. I was content. One morning I got up to go to work. As usual I picked up the baby, changed him, fixed a bottle, and played with him before putting him down in his crib. I then left for work. At about ten o'clock, I received a call to hurry home. I hurried home only to find a medical team in our home. When I entered, I saw Kenneth lying on the couch and the doctor sitting beside him. Virginia was sobbing on her knees at a chair, and a neighbor lady was standing close to Virginia. She was who had called me. The doctor looked up at me and said that Kenneth was dead—he thought from crib death. That was in March 1961. I am not sure that Virginia ever fully recovered from the trauma of loosing Kenneth.

In 1962, both my parents died, Dad of a heart attack in February and Mother in an auto accident July 1st. The loss was huge, but life must go on. I felt that I should return to college, so I made application and was accepted for the second time. I was determined to stick it out and get an education. However, things didn't work as I had planned. There were several events that hindered me from achieving my desired goal. First, my father-in-law, for whom I had so much respect, was caught up in a morals situation, and I was called back to Eagle Point to deal with that situation. The church was devastated, and he was only sorry he got caught.

I was able to get a temporary pastor to take the church, and we moved their family to Washington to be near us. My in-laws living near put a real strain on my family, and we spent too much time with them trying to bring some kind of healing. Second, there was a financial burden added to our already tight budget. Third, my wife became unhappy with where we lived and decided we needed to move into a big house that we couldn't afford. And I let her talk me into it. This all became too much for me to deal with along with school, so I dropped out.

I went to work driving a log truck for a friend who had a logging company. I was working for him when Winona Lee joined the family May 20, 1964.

That summer, Rod, the owner of the company, and Troy, my father-in-law, made a deal with a sawmill to log a section of timber that was difficult to log and was a long way from home. We stayed in a cabin in the mountains and came home on the weekends. There wasn't much money made that summer, and winter was without any work. That spring we started back to work, but the money was scarce. Virginia was at home facing all of the demands for money that we didn't have. In August I received a call that Virginia was in the hospital with a nervous breakdown. I walked away from the logging and took a job in Roseburg, Oregon.

Back In Roseburg

It seems that when my world was falling apart, I would return to my hometown to regroup. That is where most of the family was and seemed to offer some sort of support. I took a job with Roseburg Produce delivering produce. The company was owned by a man the family had known forever. I had known Bob Brown all of my life but still had to prove myself. I told him to give me a week and I would have the job down. Within the week, I had proven myself capable. That job lasted three years until I challenged him on my wages. At that point I was dismissed with a week's pay.

While in Roseburg, there was a measure of healing. Virginia wanted to go back to her home church in Myrtle Creek. I thought that was a good plan since I knew the church and liked the people there. This was a good place for me because I was under the direction of a pastor. We attended the Myrtle Creek church all of the time we lived in Roseburg. While there, I served as Sunday school teacher, youth pastor, and worship leader. I also had the opportunity to preach there and in several churches around the area.

When I was dismissed from Roseburg Produce, I was left with a wondering of what God had for me to do. No jobs seemed to open up, so I looked back to ministry. I learned of a church in Clarkston, Washington that was looking for a pastor. I applied and was accepted. We stayed there for about two and a half years. I had a lot of struggles there because of low self esteem and lack of preparation for pastoring. I lead the church in a building program but was unable to finish it. I left there defeated, I felt like a failure for not completing the building. The district office encouraged me by saying that I was not a failure and that they were happy with the work I had done. Still, I never could get past the feeling of failure.

We had a friend pastoring in California who put us in touch with a church looking for a pastor. After going down and preaching, we were voted in and served there for just over a year. I couldn't get past my failure and my lack of education really showed up. To add to my struggle, Virginia was very unhappy. Nothing pleased her; the house wasn't good enough; the church was in the wrong part of town. Nothing I did could fulfill the emptiness or unhappiness she felt. I am confident that my own struggles added to the pressure she felt.

I had been struggling with an addiction to pornography for about four years at this time. I would pray and ask God to forgive me and swear I would never go there again only to fall back into the old trap. My wife was aware of this but never said much about it. It just stayed in the background. It seemed like the material would just show up at the most unexpected places, and I would be back into it. This addiction was present during our pastorate at both churches. I knew I could not pastor and have such addiction hanging on to me. And I could not share this with anyone. As a result, the only thing left for me was to resign the ministry.

It was during this time I was at the church praying. I was praying about the church and my role there, I really needed some direction. It seemed that God spoke to me and said, “You are finished here.” I remember continuing in prayer and trying to make sense out of what I heard. The more I prayed, the more convinced I became that I had heard correctly.

I got up and went home and asked the family how they would like to go back to Roseburg. They all said they would like that. The next Sunday, I resigned with the idea that I was never going to pastor again. I told my friend, a fellow pastor, that I was never going to pastor again. I said, “I am just going to be the best layman in the church I can be,” and I was dead serious.

I have never spoken of this addiction before, however I believe it is something that I should talk about as it may help someone who may be struggling with an addiction. It seemed to start innocently enough. I would see a magazine somewhere and pick it up, look at the pictures and read some of the articles. No harm in looking. I would find different magazines in places I didn’t expect. It seemed that they would just show up. Then I started looking for them, and there were plenty of places available. As the desire became more intense, I would take the magazines and hide them so as to look at them in my leisure. Soon my wife discovered the magazines, but her only comment was, “You shouldn’t be looking at this.” I agreed but couldn’t stop.

While serving at Clarkston, I struggled with this problem, although I seemed to be able to keep it under control. I was busy enough with church work and involved in a building program. Moving to Stockton was a different scenario. I had more time, and pornography was everywhere. Soon I was in over my head and couldn’t get free even for a moment. I realized what was happening and would pray for God to clean me up and set me free, but I was hooked and this thing was out of control.

According to James Rutz, author of the book *Mega Shift*, page 120, in a survey of U.S. pastors, he lists 7 things that pastors struggle with. On the list, he states that 37% of pastors say they are currently struggling with Internet porn.

This is not just an easy way of using their spare time. It is a diabolical trick of the devil to keep pastors trapped and to render them useless to the kingdom.

Lest anyone think they are above such entrapment, remember what the apostle John wrote: "For all that *is* in the world, the lust of the flesh, and the lust of the eyes, and the pride of life, is not of the Father, but is of the world. And the world passeth away, and the lust thereof: but he that doeth the will of God abideth for ever" *(1 John 2:16-17)*. We are all subject to like passions and must guard against the tricks of our enemy.

Leaving The Ministry

We did go to Roseburg and started attending the church of my childhood. They had a good youth program, and I enjoyed the preaching. It was a good place to heal from my emotional wounds. Shortly after we started attending the Nazarene church and became comfortable with the pastor, my wife and I talked about my addiction. We decided to call the pastor and tell him about my problem and pray for deliverance. God did set me free, although I had to be very careful to not get caught back into the trap of pornography. I would find magazines from time to time, and I had to resolve not to go there. It was not easy, but God saw me through to victory.

I would like to say that whenever Satan can trap a servant of God into a secret sin, he can marginalize his ministry. That person, no matter how much they desire to have confidence in God, is trapped by the accuser and is rendered helpless to do battle with Satan.

We attended the church for nine years, and I felt my spiritual life grow as well as my emotional life. With my addiction out of the way, I started really getting involved in the church. I did become a laymen and was happy serving in whatever capacity I was asked. I took special interest in the pastor. I was like a sponge learning from him. I listened to his council to me and to others. I learned from observation. I watched how he ran a board meeting. I learned how to work with men. I soaked up everything I could from the pastor on how a church should run. It was not my intent to use any of the skills, but my heart was there and I couldn't help myself, I was fascinated by his skill. As a side note, our church was averaging over 600 at that time, and I was excited to be a part of it.

Calling God Father

I have been a Christian most of my life having asked Jesus into my heart at the age of eight. Receiving Christ at an early age does not mean you automatically mature any earlier, and it may mean that habits and insecurities lend themselves to more self reliance than trusting in God. That is where I found myself, trying to serve God in my own strength and effort. I didn't think that was the case, but who of us know our heart until God gets us to the place where we see what God sees. When we have a genuine desire to serve God, God will take us to His school teaching us His ways, thus making us useful servants.

I had gone to Bible college, served as youth minister, held regional office in the district, served as pastor, and in general served wherever I was asked. With this background, one would think that I would be well on my way to being a useful servant in God's Kingdom, but that was not the case. I had come to the end of myself. Life now was just a daily grind, and I was redirecting my focuses from ministry to making a living and serving in the local church.

I had returned to my hometown and to the church of my childhood. I returned a broken man, a failure in ministry, my marriage was in trouble, I was hooked on pornography, and financially we were just barely getting by.

As we settled into the local church, my wife and I sought help for my addiction. God broke the chains and set me free. My marriage was healed, and I was delivered from my addiction. As healing began, I felt a measure of success and started a remodeling business. I was happy to be where I was in marriage, in the church, and in business, and money was starting to come.

It was at this time as I was saying my goodnight prayers when the subject of God being my father came up. I remember God asked me if I could call Him father, I responded that I could not. He then asked me if I could call my Dad "father." I said yes. Then God asked me why I could call Dad "father" but was not able to call him "father?" I responded, "When Dad told me something, I could count on it, but I don't know that about you."

My response was startling to me; why could I call Dad "father" but was unable to call God "Father?" What was behind the inquiry, why such a question? I had often referred to God as Father in prayer and conversation. Nevertheless, there was something different that night. I was brought face to face with my independence. I was faced with the truth of who had been Lord of my life. I thought that I had totally surrendered to God everything when I invited Christ to be my savior. To discover I could not call God Father was disturbing to say the least.

This brought to the forefront the question of who was sitting on the throne of my life: was it God or was it me? Was I going to continue being in charge, or was I going to turn the control over to my Heavenly Father?

God was asking me a very penetrating question. Was our relationship superficial, and if it was, was I willing to make the necessary changes to improve our relationship? God was asking for more than just a verbal expression of saying "father." He was asking me for a deep relational commitment, one where I could call Him Father with the trust, confidence, and commitment that a "father" is entitled to.

What was usually a two minute prayer turned into a couple of hours struggling over God being my Father. It was not easy to give up my own concept of God as just a distant personage. I always knew that God was there. I had seen God's handywork in so many ways. Yet I was still holding something back. When things got tough, I would ask for God's help, but then I would figure out how to make it work on my own.

If things didn't work out, I would just resign myself to thinking, "That's the way it is," and move on with no resolution to the circumstances. I believed that God could handle some things, but there were other things He couldn't. I remember saying to a friend one time that I believed God could handle anything but financial problems. That was the area where I was having my most frustrating struggles. I could not get victory over that part of my life. I wasn't stingy, but I didn't know how to manage what little I had coming in.

Accepting Him as one that I could trust and depend upon was quite a stretch for me because for most of my life I depended on myself and what I was able to do. I trusted Dad, but I depended on me. As for my devotions, my personal life was separate from Christian life. I read the scripture regularly but read with the idea of what I could give to others. My studies were for sermons, not for personal growth. Some Scriptures I internalized, but most were used to share with others.

What God was asking of me was to give up myself, to place my total trust and confidence in Him. Quite a stretch for someone who had learned their survival skills by not making waves and trusting in his own ability. I believed in God, and I believed in His Word. I was able to believe that God was who He said He was. I believed the Scripture from cover to cover, every word as the inspired word of God. Yet I was unable to make God and His Word a personal reality in my life. My pastor said to me one day, "Glen, you know the Scriptures, but you don't believe the Scriptures." What he was saying to me was that, while I had knowledge of the Scriptures, I had not internalized them and made them my own to live by.

I had experienced a lot of life's struggles by this time in my life. A life that was supposed to be on target for success was side tracked. The things I had dedicated my life to were finished. My dreams of being a successful pastor were over. I had come to the place of melting back into the background and going to church as my only commitment to Christ. As a Christian, I was just operating in survival mode.

I knew that I could trust my Dad because I had many years of experience with him. I had watched him deal with life in its most difficult times. I had seen how much he trusted God and the scripture to sustain life for our family. When God asked me the question, it was an instant response. I had a history with Dad. I had experience and observation that I could point to. I had proof that he could be trusted. It was easy to say I could whole-heartedly call him "father."

My experience with God was not as personal as my experience with my Dad. I had received Christ as my personal savior as a youth, however, I had never learned to trust Him as a provider. I believed that God was my savior, but I felt that I had to work for Him. My greatest desire was to be of service to God, and so I put all of my energies into doing for God. I didn't think this was so, but in retrospect my life was based on works. My life centered on what I could do for God.

Oswald Chambers writes in "My Utmost for His Highest," May 31 devotional: "The purpose of our Christian training is to get into the right relationship to the 'needs' of God and His will. Once God's 'needs' in us have been met, He will open the way for us to accomplish His will, meeting His 'needs' elsewhere" *(Luke 24:49)*. I had the cart before the horse. I felt that the only way I could prove my love and commitment to God was to work for Him. Everything was measured by what I could do and how busy I was in service to God in the church and in ministry.

That night I entered into a new relationship with God. There were no bells ringing, no flashing lights, no deep emotional feelings—just an understanding that I could call God "Father." From that time God began to be a Father to me. I have learned that as Father, God is interested in His children becoming mature, and not remaining babes in Christ. Mature children learn from the things God gives them to grow by. Babies whine and complain, claiming life isn't fair. James 1:2 says, "Count it all joy when trials come your way." I have learned that every child will be tested, corrected, and run through life's proving ground to learn what is that good and perfect will of God.

I was unsure of how far I was able to trust God. I felt that I had made a total surrender, but the only way to be sure was to be tested. God has a way of testing us, to prove our commitment and to experience the hand of God in all circumstances. I like what Bill Gaither says in one of his songs: "If we never had a problem we wouldn't know that God could solve them." God as our father knows us intimately. He knows all of the areas in our life that need work, what needs pruning, and what needs to be strengthened.

God as father is interested in His children becoming fully mature and equipped for service in His vineyard. Too often, we desire God to act as a magic wand and respond to our bidding and our wishes. We expect God to respond to our needs the way our earthy father did when we were children, still adolescents and not mature. As Paul put it, babes in Christ desire milk, unable to take solid meat. This is what I call looking to God as Daddy rather than as Father.

When we think of God as Daddy, we think of a God that will take care of all of our troubles. This is what we expected from our earthly daddy. When a problem would arise, we would run to our Dad, and he would fix the problem to our satisfaction. There was nothing for us to do because Dad had the knowledge and experience to make everything right. This was not bad because it taught us to depend on him for all of our needs and to build confidence in him as our Dad. Dad could fix anything; he was stronger than any other person; he provided comfort and security in every situation. This was good when we were children because it provided a secure arena where we could explore, learn, and grow up to become mature adults.

As we matured, Dad ceased doing things for us that we could do for ourselves. He gave us chores to do and required accountability to see that the chores were done. If we had trouble, he gave guidance and encouragement. As we matured, our Dad required accountability, and when we failed to be accountable he would provide the necessary correction.

Our Heavenly Father is not so different. When we first receive Christ as our personal savior, Saint Paul describes us as new born children, babes in Christ. As new born children, we feel free, and all of our burdens are lifted from us. We feel like we can take on the whole world. There isn't anything we are unable to do. God is so real, we can trust Him for everything that comes our way. Then as we begin to mature and grow, we find things are a little more challenging. God lets us walk by ourselves. He doesn't seem as close as He did when we were first born and new. A few trials come our way—some confrontations, some issues of life that begin to surface—and we think that God isn't there anymore. We begin to question, Satan begins to accuse, and we start to doubt our relationship with God.

God wants us to grow from the daddy stage to the Father stage where we know that He is there even when we don't feel Him or think that He is there. This maturity comes over a period of time as we realize how much we are able to trust in God as Father. There are times when God will always be our Daddy, and those times are special. There are times when God wants to be Father, and these are times of growth. The more we are into the written word of God, the less we depend on our feelings or emotions. Feelings and emotions are good, but we cannot depend on them, however we can always depend on the word of God.

The more we matured, the less our Dad did for us and the more we went to him with bigger problems, seeking his council on how to deal with the challenges that we encountered. There was never a time that we did not believe he would be there when we needed him. As we mature in Christ, we find that God deals with us in much the same way. When God asked me if I could call him Father, He was asking for a mature response, one that was not a "Daddy, fix it." God wanted to know if I truly trusted Him for all of life's needs and struggles. When I compared my confidence in God as compared to my confidence in my Dad, I had to admit that I didn't have as much trust in God as I did in Dad.

Little was I to know what steps God would take me through to prove my trust, not only in Him, but to myself. A Father's relationship is a deeper relationship than a Daddy relationship. A Daddy's relationship is to provide comfort and to make sure that you have all of the necessary things for living at the stage of life where you are. A Father's job is to train, give instruction, offer guidance, and develop maturity so that no matter what comes or what we face in life, we will be able to handle it with confidence. Paul said "When I was a child I spoke as a child, I thought as a child, I acted as a child, but when I became a man I put away childish things" *(1 Cor. 13:11)*.

The purpose of the Father is to help us put away childish things. God wants His children to become mature Christians. He wants us to grow in faith, a total trust in Him. The problem God had with Israel was they continued to turn to other gods for answers rather than follow God's instructions. When God brought the children of Israel out of Egypt, God did everything for them, but when they were left alone for just a short time, they returned to the gods of the past. Are we any different? When we no longer feel the presence of God, we return to our old way of coping. I must confess, although I had received Christ as a child, I depended on God only when I could feel the presence of God. When things were tough and I was left to my own, I did what I thought was right, trusting in my own judgment and not waiting on God or even asking what He would have me do.

When God says something to us, He wants us to trust Him to bring it to pass. He wants us to trust Him for all of life's challenges. When we do, we can rest in God and know that everything will work out for the best no matter how dark or bleak things look. I think of the song:

> *What a friend we have in Jesus all our sins and grief's to bare. What a privilege to carry everything to God in prayer. Oh what peace we often forfeit, oh what*

> *needless pain we bare. All because we do not carry everything to God in prayer.*
>
> *And we know that all things work together for good to them that love God, to them who are called according to his purpose (Romans 8:28).*

The Father wants his children to trust His judgment even when they don't understand the path He has chosen for them to follow. I think of Paul when God said, "I will show him what great things he must suffer for my name sake." When He told Joshua "be not afraid" seven times in the first chapter of Joshua. When He told Gideon to reduce his troops to three hundred. When He told Peter that it doesn't matter what the other disciples do, you follow me. And when he told me that He was not going to deliver me from the financial collapse I was facing.

We want to trust God when He is Daddy to us, but we don't want to trust God when He is teaching, training, disciplining, or is silent; when we are left to trust only in Him and His word and don't have a clue as to what is ahead of us; when our world crumbles around us, our health fails, our marriage falls apart, or we lose our job. Are we able to say, like Job, "Even though He slay me, yet will I trust Him" *(Job 13:15)*?

needless pain we bare. All because we do not carry everything to God in prayer.

And we know that all things work together for good to them that love God, to them who are called according to his purpose (Romans 8:28).

The Father wants his children to trust His judgment even when they don't understand the path He has chosen for them to follow. I think of Paul when God said, "I will show him what great things he must suffer for my name sake." When He told Joshua "be not afraid" seven times in the first chapter of Joshua. When He told Gideon to reduce his troops to three hundred. When He told Peter that it doesn't matter what the other disciples do, you follow me. And when he told me that He was not going to deliver me from the financial collapse I was facing.

We want to trust God when He is Daddy to us, but we don't want to trust God when He is teaching, training, disciplining, or is silent; when we are left to trust only in Him and His word and don't have a clue as to what is ahead of us; when our world crumbles around us, our health fails, our marriage falls apart, or we lose our job. Are we able to say, like Job, "Even though He slay me, yet will I trust Him" *(Job 13:15)*?

The Dark Time

At this time I was in business for myself. I had started a home improvement remolding and construction company. For the first couple of years, things flourished. I felt God's hand was on me and was content at what I was doing. We were able to buy a home on the river. We bought a new car and work truck. I was able to add to my tools and employ several employees. As a bonus, I bought 40 acres in the country with plans to build a future home and other property with rentals and space to build a commercial warehouse. I used part of the warehouse for my business and rented the rest to another business.

I felt God's blessing on everything, and the future looked bright. Then our world changed. In 1979 and 1980, the economy took a huge downward turn, and I was caught in the spiral.

By 1980, I was trying to keep things afloat by robbing Paul to pay Peter. I was also serving as mission's president of the church, and the pastor suggested I go to Guatemala with a team to build a church there. Things were tight, but my way was paid, so I agreed to go. I had a new building nearly completed and left instructions to complete it while I was gone. When I returned, the building was not only not completed, but some other issues had arisen that were costing me money I didn't have. Finally, the building was completed to everyone's satisfaction, but new work was not coming in. I had expenses that did not stop just because the work slowed down. We sold our home on the river, sold the 40 acres, and moved into one of the rental houses. That was still not enough to keep ahead of the expenses.

Things were really squeezing me, and I didn't have any answers. At that time, I talked with our pastor, and he suggested that I take my wife and go to the coast for a few days and get away from everything and relax. I took his advice, and we went to the coast. Virginia and I had a few days of relaxing and enjoying the coast. While there, I was also praying about our situation at home. I really needed some help. I remember praying, and I was never so sincere in my life. I told God that I wanted Him to reveal himself to me in such a way that there could be no doubt that it was God. I shared my prayer with Virginia. She didn't have much to say, probably didn't know how to respond. When we returned home, I was all excited because God was going to turn everything around and life would be good again.

That did not happen. Things continued to go downhill. It was like I had a huge tent over me. When one side would start to fall, I would grab a prop and run there and prop up what was falling. Then another area would start to fall and I would take the prop from where I had it and prop up that area. This game of prop switching continued for several months. My business was broke, and I had very little money coming in from jobs. It seemed like someone had thrown the switch and turned the jobs off. Things stopped overnight, and there was no work to be had.

I remember spending many nights lying on the floor in the living room praying for God to supply money to pay my bills, but none came. We cut back everywhere we could, but that was not enough. I remember driving out to the shop one day and saying to God, "God, you have got to do something about this." I was talking about paying my creditors. God spoke to me just as clearly as I have ever heard anyone speak. He said, "And what are you going to do if I don't?" Talk about a setback, I was stunned. I thought for a moment and laughed and said, "I will trust you anyway." What else could I do?

I went home and told Virginia that I had put my last prop up. If it fell, it fell. And boy did it fall. I wound up in bankruptcy and lost my buildings and my property. I thought, "What about God showing himself to me in such a way that there could be no doubt?" I didn't question, but I wondered how this could be of God. God was still God, and I determined to trust him even when I couldn't see the path ahead of me.

We moved to California for a few years, and I worked. But I couldn't make enough to pick up and start over. I became discouraged, and my esteem took another huge hit. Virginia was very unhappy with where we lived. It was a nice place, but she wanted to move after a year or so, and that cost us more money that we didn't have. I was fighting for my life emotionally and financially. Everything I tried seemed to not quite be enough to turn things around.

During this time, my older brother stopped by to visit and left before I got home from work. He was on his way to Colorado. When I got home, Virginia told me that Joe and his wife had stopped. They wanted to see me but didn't want to wait. I thought that was okay. I wasn't accustomed to family stopping anyway.

About an hour later, Joe and his wife returned and said they felt that they could not go on without seeing me. After we visited for some time, he told me that he had gone to Alaska and was driving truck for Bud Glenn. Bud was a friend who had a business in Winston, Oregon, but had gone to Alaska when things went bad in Oregon. Joe said he was going to get his own truck and not drive for Bud the next year.

I said, "Do you think I could drive for Bud?" and he thought I probably could. I turned to Virginia and said, "We are going to Alaska."

Within a month, we had emptied a four bedroom home. We took only what we could fit into the back of a pickup truck and headed for Alaska.

Sometimes when a person is in the midst of a storm, they can't see the hand of God even when it is present. When things went bad in Oregon and I didn't have anywhere to turn, how is it that I had made contact with a friend in California and I was able to go right to work? How is it that we were able to move into a very nice place with reasonable rent? How is it that Joe felt the need to return and spend the night? How is it that I knew Bud and believed I could go to work for him? How is it that we felt such peace about making such a move? How is it that we were able to sell everything in such a short time and be ready to make the move within a month? When I look back, I can see the hand of God in it all, even though I still didn't see an end to the financial struggle.

In the midst of all of the struggles, there were several Scriptures that were constant in my mind. I quoted them daily and thought about them at night. This seemed to be the only source of stability I could find. I didn't see any results from the scripture, but that didn't mean to me that they were not true and that someday God would answer. The Scriptures were:

> *Joshua 1:8 This book of the law shall not depart out of thy mouth; but thou shalt meditate therein day and night, that thou mayest observe to do according to all that is written therein: for then thou shalt make thy way prosperous, and then thou shalt have good success.*

9 Have not I commanded thee? Be strong and of a good courage; be not afraid, neither be thou dismayed: for the LORD thy God is with thee whithersoever thou goest. (KJ)

Psalms 1:1 Blessed is the man that walketh not in the counsel of the ungodly, nor standeth in the way of sinners, nor sitteth in the seat of the scornful.

2 But his delight is in the law of the LORD; and in his law doth he meditate day and night.

3 And he shall be like a tree planted by the rivers of water, that bringeth forth his fruit in his season; his leaf also shall not wither; and whatsoever he doeth shall prosper. (KJ)

Mathew 5:6 Blessed are they which do hunger and thirst after righteousness: for they shall be filled. (KJ)

Mathew 6: 33 But seek ye first the kingdom of God, and his righteousness; and all these things shall be added unto you. (KJ)

Malachi 3:10 Bring ye all the tithes into the storehouse, that there may be meat in mine house, and prove me now herewith, saith the LORD of hosts, if I will not open you the windows of heaven, and pour you out a blessing, that there shall not be room enough to receive it.

11 And I will rebuke the devourer for your sakes, and he shall not destroy the fruits of your ground; neither shall your vine cast her fruit before the time in the field, saith the LORD of hosts. (KJ)

Glen's family: David, Gwendolyn, Virginia, Glen, Winona (Windy) 1981

The Silent Years

We arrived in Alaska the spring of 1984. That summer I went to work on a paving crew driving a dump truck. I wanted to learn to operate the roller and so stayed after work and watched the roller operator and rode the roller with him. By the middle of summer, I secured the job as roller operator. I loved the job and made more money than I had for several years. Everything stopped when things froze up at the end of October. I was out of work until the next spring.

The next spring, I went to work for a lumber company for half the pay I had been making with the paving company. However the work was year-round, and I was able to work through the next winter.

We went to different churches but didn't seem to connect with any. I read my Bible, but not every day. I was disappointed that I had lost everything. My confidence was shattered; my credit was destroyed; Virginia was having a lot of health problems with her heart and eyes. I began to drift spiritually and didn't seem to care. What was the use? There didn't seem to be any answers. Church was okay but didn't seem to reach me. Although we continued to attend, I felt empty. Later we moved to Anchorage, and I worked for another lumber company. I liked the job, and the pay was good. I stayed with that job until the store where I worked closed. At that time, we decided to move back to the lower forty-eight.

In Anchorage, we attended the Nazarene Church. I liked the pastor and we got involved working in the church. I served on the board as Christian Life Director. I was developing a series of classes on self esteem. I taught that class for several quarters and gave a class for the Alaska State Sunday School Convention held annually in Anchorage. I felt a measure of success, but that was short lived. I think I was still chasing a dream.

While in Alaska, Virginia and I were having our problems. She was not happy with me, and I was not happy with her. I felt she was using her sickness to control me, and I don't know what she thought. I think she felt that I was not compassionate or didn't care about her health. The truth is I was worn out. I was tired of the struggle.

When we moved out of Alaska, I took a job logging in California and worked until the season closed.

Then we moved in with her parents for a while in Medford, Oregon. We had no idea where we were going to settle or how. It seemed that God was nowhere to be found, and I was sure He didn't care either. A short while after we were with her folks, she told me that she was going back to Alaska to live with our daughter and her sisters and I could do what I wanted to. I took her to the airport and saw her off to Alaska. As I drove away, I felt like the whole world was lifted from me. I felt free.

When You Think God Is Not Working, Think Again

I drove to Redmond, Oregon and went on a sales trip with my older brother. The trip took us through a town in Washington where I had been stationed while in the service. I called an old friend, and we had breakfast with him and a good visit. He asked me what I was doing and I related what I had been doing and that I had nothing lined up for the future.

He said, "Buy my business. I want to retire." He had a floor covering business installing carpet and vinyl. He said he would teach me the trade and sell me all the tools and equipment. I thanked him and said I would think about it, but I really wasn't interested. I knew nothing about that kind of work.

On the way back to Redmond, Joe and I were talking about different things, and the offer came up. I said, "You know that might be a good deal in Moses Lake."

He said, "I was just thinking that also."

When we got back to Redmond, I didn't have any place to go. I didn't want to go back to Virginia's parents, and I didn't want to live in the back of my pickup truck. I called Clayton and said I would come up and look at what he had to offer and make a decision.

The next day I drove back to Moses Lake and stayed a few days with Clayton. I went out on a couple of jobs and thought I could learn the trade. I decided to buy his business with no money but lots of hard work.

One day a lady that owned a business we installed for asked me, "Did you know anything about installation, or did you just jump in blind, dumb, and happy?"

I told her that I had jumped in blind, dumb, and happy. She laughed, and I installed for her as long as I was in the business.

With Virginia in Alaska, I felt free to make the decision to buy the business and move to Moses Lake. A place for me to rent was also available for very reasonable rent. It wasn't much of a place, but it was fine for me, which is all I had to worry about. We had shipped our furniture down from Alaska with some friends who had moved the same time that we left Alaska. The furniture was in storage in the Seattle area. Clayton gave me the use of a trailer and extra storage, so I was able to bring everything to Moses Lake and set up housekeeping for myself.

I settled into my new life and new job quickly. I attended church but did not get involved. I had had all of church work I needed and was not interested in serving in any way. I did keep my Bible handy and read the scripture often. For me life could not have been better. I was rebuilding my life after losing everything in Roseburg.

Virginia seemed to be happy in Alaska and started taking some schooling to help her find work. I went up to see her once, and we had a good time, but I think she was glad to see me go back to Moses Lake. After about six months, she called and said school was too stressful and she couldn't keep up with the class. She asked if she could come back, and I said that would be fine. She was back in my life again. I knew that I would have to take care of her because she was unable to function on her own. I was good with that. For the next several years, we were together and our relationship grew stronger and became better with each year. I am so glad we made it work.

We stayed in Moses Lake for nine years, and I enjoyed the business. We were feeling some success with our finances, but the rest of my life was on hold. I didn't think about spiritual things much, although we were faithful to church. We were bench warmers at best.

During this time, I was reading the scripture, and a couple of verses spoke to me. I made an appointment with the pastor and shared the scripture with him. His comment was, "It looks like God is saying something to you." I didn't think so, but I was open to God. The Scriptures were found in Hosea. I copied them down on a card and carried them in my Bible for several years.

> *Hosea 10:12 Sow for yourselves righteousness, reap the fruit of unfailing love, and break up your unplowed ground; for it is time to seek the LORD, until he comes and showers righteousness on you.*

> *Hosea 14:3 Assyria cannot save us; we will not mount war-horses. We will never again say 'Our gods' to what our own hands have made, for in you the fatherless find compassion.*

The first scripture seemed to say, "You have been unfruitful long enough. It is time to get serious about the work of the Lord." Although I had no idea what I could do or even wanted to do.

The second scripture seemed to say, "You have trusted in your ability long enough. It is time to put your total trust in God." Sounds good, but I was not interested in any changes in my life or changes in location. I was content to be in Moses Lake and enjoying my business; and for me life couldn't have been better.

God Began To Move Us Out From Moses Lake

First: My body began to say, "You can't keep the pace of installing floors anymore." I was getting too slow to be profitable, and my strength was fading to the point it was taking all that I could do to finish a job.

Second: I was offered a job as setup manager for a manufactured home company. I did well at that job, but the pay was not good enough to meet all of our needs. I was supposed to be able to work extra to make more money, but that didn't happen.

Third: The home we had been renting for the past five years with the thought of buying fell through, and we had to move into an apartment.

Fourth: My older brother invited me to Alaska to visit and while there persuaded me that I should move back to Alaska as there were better opportunities for me there.

Fifth: When I returned to Moses Lake, I told the man I worked for that I planned to move to Alaska and would be leaving the end of May. He terminated me as of the end of April.

Sixth: Virginia was good with the move.

For the second time, we had a big sale and sold most of the things we had acquired. Taking what we could haul in a van and pickup, we headed for Alaska.

The Long Road Back

As we were closing up our affairs in Moses Lake, Virginia flew to Fairbanks to be with her sisters. I loaded the vehicles and first drove the van, towing our car to Alaska. I later came back and drove the pickup to Alaska.

The trip to Alaska was a weeklong trip, and I had a lot of time to think. Along the trip, I began to think about ministry and what I could do. For my part, I was washed up and of no use to God or myself. I remember talking to God during the trip. At one point in order to make myself feel like I was not being disobedient to the call, I told God, "I will go back into the ministry, but I will not seek it. If you want me there, you will have to put me there."

That settled the question because I knew God would not put me in the ministry. I had several years behind me to prove my point. I genuinely was wanting to follow what God wanted for my life, but I had no desire to pursue any type of ministry.

I was in Alaska for nine years during which God slowly and methodically turned my life around and placed me in ministry.

First: We started attending a community nondenominational church. I had met the pastor and his wife while visiting Alaska in the spring just before our move. No real draw, but I liked them. The church was meeting in a school with hopes of building a place of worship sometime in the future. The people were friendly, but I wasn't. I wanted to be left alone and come to church and leave with no attachment.

Second: I was working on a job in Anchorage doing a remodel on an apartment building. The man I was working for and I went to lunch. When we returned, I had a medical appointment and was ready to leave when he asked me to help him load some material into the back of the apartment building. Leaving the keys in the van, I went to help. When I returned from helping him, my van was gone with all of my tools. I was devastated. We immediately notified the police. I thought the van would be found because there were only minutes between the time the van was taken and it was reported.

I could not see how this could be of God even though I left the keys in the van. I could not ask for God's help because of my actions. Little did I know how that event would work to guide me in the direction God had for me to follow.

Third: With the van and my tools all gone, I was left with "What do I do now?" I did some work for a contactor in the valley, but that didn't last. I began to ask myself, "What could I do?" It was at this time I thought about education again. I asked Virginia what she thought about me going back to school and becoming a counselor. She thought that would be a good idea. So I began to look for a school.

I checked into a private Christian college because I thought it would be easier to get into. The cost was prohibitive. Next, I went to the University of Alaska and asked to see a counselor. I was seen by a man who was very helpful. I told him I had dropped out of school in the ninth grade and had been faking an education all of my adult life. I didn't tell him that I had attended two and a half years at a private Christian college. I also told him that I just wanted to know if I could do the work. He laid out a plan for me and said I would have to take some test, but he thought I would do fine. Also, as a senior over sixty I could get a tuition waver. All I would have to pay was for books and labs.

School was good, and I did enjoy the classes. My grades were good, and I really picked up a lot from each class. I got along well with both the students and teachers, and my self esteem was beginning to come back. I even began to think that I might be of some use to God, perhaps in the counseling field.

At the close of spring semester of 2002, I received a letter from the National Dean's List honoring America's outstanding college students. The letter said, "Congratulation. You have been selected to receive an honorary award recognition." There was more to the letter that spoke of the honor that this was and that I could be published in the Annual Edition of The National Deans List, 2001-2002. I thought this was a joke, and all they were after was to suck me into buying their book and spending money. I later learned that this was no joke and the college actually had nominated me. I did feel honored, especially when I learned that only ½ of 1% of the nation's college students received this award. To me this was a testimony of the blessing of God and a confirmation that I was not as dumb as my third grade teacher made me out to be.

As summer approached, I needed something to do. I saw a Princess Tour bus and thought, "That looks like it would be a good summer job." I called the company and was told that training started in February. This was late March, so I said, "Well it looks like I am too late."

I was told, "Not necessarily," and they sent me a application. I filled it out and took it in because I wanted to see the people and I wanted them to see me. I was impressed with what I saw but was unsure what they thought. I no sooner got home from taking in the application when I received a phone call asking me when I could come in for an interview.

I interviewed and got the job. I loved the work, I loved driving, and I enjoyed the tourists. For me this was the job I had always wanted. It was fun, and I interacted with all kinds of people from all over the world. I was able to go on tour with the tourists and get paid for it. I studied the tour manuals and learned as much about Alaska as I could. This gave me information to give an informative tour, and I liked to mix it with humor to give the tourists as good a time in Alaska as possible.

I felt like God had finally smiled on me, and I was soaking it up. I drove a bus for seven years and enjoyed the experience. As time went along, God began to move me into another direction with Him. There were times that I was driving alone from one point to another. During these times, my mind would always go to spiritual things. I did not desire anything special, just a closer relationship with God. Many times as I would be driving I would sing a little chorus that became a prayer. I would pray this prayer over and over without trying to figure out how God would work. I was open to however He chose to draw me closer to Him. The words were, "Whatever it takes to draw closer to you Lord, that's what I'd be willing to do".

After my fifth year of driving, I was starting to lose the enthusiasm for the job that I had in the beginning. I still enjoyed the work, but other things began to surface that took my mind away from touring. We moved my in-laws in with us, and they stayed for about four months before they could get into their own place. I was still attending classes at the university and driving part-time.

The church we were attending was in a building program. They were developing 40 acres and building a new church on part of the parcel next to the highway. I thought this was great. I supported the pastor in his ministry and encouraged him all I could to keep up the good fight. The church was not connected to any organization; therefore the pastor did not have any outside source of encouragement when things became overwhelming.

The pastor and I met every week for several weeks. The pastor was struggling with people getting upset and leaving the church. There seemed to be quite a bit of dissention over the youth program and things in general. I encouraged him to hang in because all churches go through times of struggle when they are growing. Satan is not going to sit by and not do all he can to interrupt the work God is doing.

I had no desire or interest in becoming part of the leadership in the church. I was content to be an encourager to the pastor and attend the church on Sundays. The church finished their building program just as the tourist season was coming to an end. There was a lot of excitement in the congregation, and things looked great for the future. At this time I was approached about becoming an elder in the church and serving as associate pastor. I didn't feel spiritually fit for such an assignment but agreed to pray about it.

After prayer and asking God, "Are you sure you want me in this position?" I agreed to become the associate pastor. I still didn't feel spiritual enough, but if God could use me and make me fit, then I was good with it—although I didn't want to do very much, just be a supporter of the pastor and other church leaders. In November of 2003, I was installed as an elder and associate pastor. Little was I to know what lay ahead of me and what role I would play in the church.

Being Thrust Back Into The Ministry

That Christmas, Virginia and I went to Idaho to spend the holidays with our family. That turned out to be the last time our family was all together. When we returned to Palmer, we returned to a hornets' nest. The pastor was involved in a morals issue, and some of the people were calling for his head on a platter. I was not prepared for what was to take place.

When the youth pastor and I received the call to meet with the pastor and he shared his failure, I went into shock. The youth minister and I were left to pick up the pieces. At that time, the church did not have a church board and everything was left to the two of us to make all decisions concerning the church and the future of the pastor.

My first move was to hit the altar and make sure that I had a right relationship with God. I then told the other elder that we were not going to make any changes in the structure of the service or church. Next we were going to wait on God to give us the direction we were to move in. As an independent church, we did not have the privilege of a district superintendent to call on for help and guidance. We could not call for a temporary pastor to fill in until we could sort things out. The only place we could go was to God, and that is where I went.

The pastor was extremely remorseful and wanted to do whatever the church decided was the correct action for such an offence. He was willing to submit to any discipline the church deemed necessary. He wrote a letter to every church in the valley. He explained his offence and asked forgiveness. His attitude was entirely different from that of the last time I had to deal with a morals issue in a church.

The youth pastor was young and had grand ideas about becoming the pastor. I did not have a problem with that since I did not want the job; however, that was not God's plan. It soon became evident that God was moving in a different direction. There was also a faction in the church that wanted to control things, and they were using the youth pastor to achieve their desired goal. It seemed that God had dumped me there blind, dumb, and not so happy.

I was sure I didn't want to be the pastor, but God had a different plan. After several months of struggle, and I mean struggle, I agreed to serve as pastor. This was the hardest time of my life stepping into shoes I felt I was not prepared to fill and preaching messages that took me all week to prepare. Every Sunday was a struggle because I never knew what waited me at each service. I would spend hours in prayer asking God for direction for every step the church took to rebuild their shattered lives. Working with the former pastor and his wife to rebuild their shattered lives and restore him spiritually, mentally, and emotionally. Bringing him back into full forgiveness and restoration.

We went through about two month of a real power struggle in which God gave me specific directions for what to do and what steps to take to hold things together. Also suddenly all of the things I had learned in Roseburg began to come into play. Without all that I had soaked up from our pastor in Roseburg, I would have been totally lost. To elaborate on the exact steps taken would be too lengthy and would not add anything. During this time, I would spend hours in prayer, and God would wake me up between three and five in the morning to give me instructions. Everything God told me to do worked out just as He said it would even when it looked impossible. The scripture that was my guiding light was:

> *Eph. 6:10 Finally, my brethren, be strong in the Lord, and in the power of his might.*
>
> *11 Put on the whole armour of God, that ye may be able to stand against the wiles of the devil.*
>
> *12 For we wrestle not against flesh and blood, but against principalities, against powers, against the rulers of the darkness of this world, against spiritual wickedness in high places.*

I realized we were in a spiritual battle, and our true enemy was Satan and not the people he was manipulating. My council to those who were caught up in the battle was, "You don't fight Satan using Satan's tools." We must use the scripture and remember our fight is with Satan, not the people that are being used by him. In the midst of this, we were able to install a board and a secretary and develop a structure for the church to function in. The desire of the church was to restore the pastor spiritually and help bring healing to him, his wife and family. Not an easy task.

There was one particular time that I really felt like God had led me down a wrong path. It was after most of the trouble subsided and a board was installed. The people that decided to stay with the church were settling in and those who decided to go to another church had left. The board and I planned a church meeting to bring everyone up-to-date as to what was going on. The meeting was set, and everyone was notified. At the time of the meeting, all of the people that had left the church showed up and for two hours took the board and me to task, telling us all of the things we were doing wrong. This was not a friendly meeting, and the board and I were not given any consideration. In fact we were the enemy.

They kept saying they wanted the youth pastor to be the pastor. Interestingly, most of the people had left before the youth pastor decided that he didn't want to stay. He had emptied his office and had not been in church for several Sundays. After about two hours of being told how we were not listening to them, I was able to bring the meeting to a close. The youth pastor was present and sat in the back and seemed to be quite pleased with everything, although he never said anything or entered into the discussion. There seemed to be a lot of anger and most of it was directed at me. The board had scheduled another meeting for the following evening, and I told the youth pastor to be at that meeting. In my heart, I was finished. I didn't want the job, and it seemed the people didn't want me.

The next morning, I went into Anchorage to tell Princess Tours that the church had found a pastor and I would take all the work they could give me. On the way into town, I began to talk to God and expressed how I felt. I said, "I think I feel like you betrayed me." I told God how I had done everything exactly as He told me, and then I said, "No, I don't think, I do feel like you betrayed me." Needless to say, my emotions were very close to the surface, and I cried a lot. I would not answer my cell phone. As far as I was concerned, the church had a pastor, and it wasn't me. I was through with the whole thing.

That afternoon at home, I did receive a call from one of the board, he said, "You haven't quit, have you?"

Fighting back the tears, I said, "We'll talk about it."

Again he said, "You haven't quit have you? You can't quit."

I responded, "We'll talk about it." The conversation ended with me saying I would be at the meeting that evening.

I expected to turn everything over to the youth pastor and walk away. The youth pastor never showed up at the meeting, and the board confirmed that I was to be the pastor, like it or not. I discovered that God had not betrayed me. Everything was done to establish the work that God wanted done: to save the church, to restore the pastor, and to bring healing. From that time on, we began to work on restoring the pastor and bringing healing to him and his family.

The board put together a process whereby the pastor could be restored. He had to stand before the church and make a public confession and ask their forgiveness. He had to seek marriage counseling for he and his wife. He had to be faithful to church but was not allowed to participate in any type of ministry. He agreed to all of the requirements the board had put in place. And for weeks he came and sat with the congregation, just being one of them. The pastor was incredibly gifted in music. For him to sit and not be able to lead worship was very difficult because that was the yearning of his heart.

After six months, we slowly began to bring him back into music, first playing the piano and then leading worship. After about a year, we started to work him into other ministry and preaching.

As time passed, things seemed to smooth out, but I was still having my early morning talks with God. I needed a lot of help. We didn't have a district that we could call on for help and direction. God was the only place I could turn.

It was during one of my early morning sessions with God when we were discussing a problem. I don't remember what, but it seemed like as He was leaving the room He stopped, turned around, and said, "Oh, by the way, you are going to get a house today. It is going to be in Palmer, and it will have a view of the mountains." We had been trying to find a house for months, but all doors seemed closed.

That day, Virginia and I were to have lunch with a board member to discuss some of the struggles the church was having. Virginia wanted to know if I was going alone or if the board was behind us. About ten in the morning, I received a call from a realtor, and he said he had a house to show us in Palmer. I told him we were going to be in Palmer for a luncheon appointment and we could meet him after lunch. He agreed to meet us. After lunch, we got into his car and drove about ten blocks to a nice neighborhood and pulled up in front of a nice three-bedroom house that had a view of the mountains with a fenced yard and a two car garage. We walked through the house and left in not more than ten minutes. As we drove away, I told the realtor that we would make an offer and see what developed.

The realtor later told me, "I never saw anyone buy a house so fast before."

When God told me we were going to get a house in Palmer and it was going to have a view of the mountains, why wait? We closed on the house in mid-May and moved in.

Virginia had been ill for several years with heart problems. Things were not getting better. Shortly after moving into our home in Palmer, she made several trips to the hospital and was in the ICU. While there, as we talked, she asked me how I felt about all of this. That was code for, "I am about to die. How do you feel about it?"

My response was, “I want God’s will to be done, because if I have my will and it doesn’t go the way I want, then I will be mad.”

She looked way off into the distance like she was looking a million miles away and then said “I like that”.

Interestingly, we moved into our new home in mid-May 2004, and on July 6, 2004, Virginia died of heart failure.

I was still pastor, and I wondered what God had in mind because I sure didn’t know the future. The only thing I knew for sure was that God was in control of my life and the future of the church.

I was still driving for Princess Tours because the church had no money for a pastor. As long as I was pastor, I never received any salary and did not expect to. After Virginia passed, I don’t know how I functioned. It was kind of a blur. The church was very helpful in many ways, and I stayed busy.

God Provides A Wife

After several months, I was praying about my life and not looking for anything particular. I began to think about marriage. I immediately put it out of my mind, saying it was too soon. A few days later, I found my mind returning to the subject of marriage, and I thought it must be okay or I would not be thinking that way. So I said to myself, "What kind of a woman would I be interested in?" As I thought about what I would want in a wife, the thought came, "Write it down." I emphatically said, "I am not writing it down."

A few weeks later, I was in a restaurant and I overheard a couple at the next table talking. The lady said to the man, "If you take me, you take my baggage."

I said to myself, "I am not taking any baggage," and I took out a piece of paper and jotted down ten things. To my surprise, I had peace and was able to put my mind at rest about looking for a wife.

It was sometime after this that God spoke to me in one of my early morning sessions and said, "I have a wife for you." I took God at His word and was perfectly content to leave it with Him.

About the same time that God said, "I have a wife for you," God said, "Glen, your financial worries are over."

As for my financial struggles, I had been struggling for most of my married life with a few periods of reprieve scattered here and there. I didn't doubt God, but thought I would have to be very careful with what money I received. I was careful, and God gave me more than enough so as not to be concerned.

Developing friendships over the years is something God uses to accomplish His will. The years that we were in Roseburg, we made some lifelong friends. Even though we were not close geographically, often going years without communicating. Still when the opportunity presented itself, it was as though we were never apart. Such was the case as to how I made contact with Donna.

When Virginia passed, the children and I agreed to send her remains back to Oregon where her parents and our son are buried. Several months after the memorial, I decided to journey to Oregon to see the grave and complete my closure. On my way back to Seattle to catch my flight home, I stopped in Salem and called some old friends that then lived in Battle Ground, Washington. We arranged to meet for lunch as I passed through. I had not talked with Dave and Virginia for several years, I don't remember how long. Anyway, we had a delightful time visiting about old times and catching up on life.

As we were ending our time together, Virginia said, "You know, Donna lives in Salem."

I responded, "Donna who?"

She said, "Donna Bishop."

When she said Donna Bishop, my heart did a little jump, and I responded casually, "Oh, that's nice." When she said Donna Bishop, I knew that Donna must still be single. Donna was one of the group that we had associated with while in Roseburg. I knew that Donna was single in Roseburg, and since she had the same last name meant that she was still single. Donna and my wife, Virginia, were friends, and our children were in school together. I had not seen or heard anything about her for about 25 years.

Virginia then said, "Would it be all right if Donna called you?"

I said sure. But she never called.

God works in mysterious ways, His wonders to perform. Donna related to me that the week before I met with Dave and Virginia that she had made contact with them. Donna said that she got out of church, and it was such a beautiful day she decided to call them and drove from Salem to Battle Ground to spend the afternoon. She said that she had not called or seen them for about fourteen years. Just a whim? I don't think so.

A couple of months later, I called Dave and Virginia and visited for a while and then asked if they had Donna's address. They did and gave it to me. I picked out a very nice card. Just kidding. I had a card in my office. I don't know where it came from, however, it said on the outside, "How are you? I am fine." Open it up, and the words were, "That about sums it up." I did add a line at the bottom saying it would be nice to hear from you and mailed it. I did not hear anything for several weeks and dismissed it thinking I wasn't going to.

Then on a Wednesday evening about 6:30, the phone rang and it was Donna. I was glad to receive her call, and we talked for a few minutes when I began to think I must end this conversation and get to church. Bible study started at 7:00, so I came up with a clever statement that I thought would allow me to say I needed to go to Bible study.

So I said, "When are you coming up?"

Her response blew my strategy out the window. She said, "When do you want me?" That completely caught me off guard.

Then my response even took me more by surprise. I said "tomorrow," and then I thought, "Where did that come from?" The end result was that we laughed and ended the conversation and I went off to Bible study.

The next day, I called my sister, who lived in Anchorage, and told her that I had invited this lady up to Alaska for a visit, but I only had a three week period that I could entertain her. I had a church conference to attend, and as soon as I returned from the conference, I started spring driver training.

My sister said, "Well call her and be honest."

I thought, "What a novel idea." I secured a nice B&B for Donna to stay at while she was visiting. I then called Donna. Donna had called on Wednesday. I talked with my sister on Thursday and called Donna back on Friday. The conversation went something like this:

"Donna, at the risk of sounding over anxious, I only have this time frame that I will be able to spend with you."

We talked, and she asked how long she should stay, and I suggested a week. About two hours later, Donna called and said, "At the risk of sounding over-anxious, I have my tickets."

Three months later, we were married in Alaska.

Glen & Donna's wedding picture 2005

When we allow our Heavenly Father to put together a program, it is perfect in every way. God not only gave me a wife, He also added a wonderful family. Our family has grown from each having three children. Now we have six. God has so blessed us in blending our family in such a way that I could not think of not having all of us together. God not only brought blessing to me and my family, he also brought blessing to Donna and her family. Our blended family has truly been a blessing to us all.

Glen & Donna's family 2015
Standing: Wendy, Becki, Bonnie, David, Gwen, Winona
Sitting: Glen & Donna

I was still pastor, and the church went all out to give us a grand wedding. It was as though God had smiled on us and blessed our union. We continued to pastor for the next year, at which time we were able to bring the pastor back into full restoration. The church was moving on in a positive way. The pastor and church were progressing in harmony. Donna and I began to feel God was leading us in another direction. Although we had no idea where or what was ahead for us.

Move To Orient

With the church moving in a good direction, I began to relax and devoted more time to driving for Princess Tours. The pastor was taking more of the responsibilities, and I was stepping back to give him space to function on his own.

One day, I received a call from my oldest sister, Polly, who was living in The Dalles, Oregon. She had moved there to be close to her daughter after her husband passed.

Polly was a former member of the Orient Community Church in Orient, Washington. She still kept in contact with all of her friends in Orient and followed the progress of the church. She told me that she had talked with Linda Morton, who was a leader in the church, and discovered that the church had gone through a split and most of the congregation had left.

At that time in her conversation with Linda, Polly said, "You know, my brother took a church in Alaska that was going through a tough time, and he brought it out."

To which Linda said, "Do you think he would come here?"

Polly said, "I don't know, but you can call him," and gave her my phone number.

She then said I possibly would receive a call from Linda. I did not take it seriously and dismissed the idea right away.

I think it was about a month later that I was surprised by a call from Linda asking if we would be interested in coming down to minister to the church. I told her that I was committed until the end of September but would come down after the tourist season ended. I was still working for Princess Tour Co. I said I would give the church two weeks to evaluate us and for us to look at the situation there.

At the end of September, Donna and I made arrangements to go to Orient. I had been there when my sister lived in the community, so I knew what to expect, but Donna had never been there. I knew Orient being a rural community could be quite a shock. The community consisted of a post office, general store, a church, and a school, with a population of about 100. The area was mostly farming, logging, and retirees located 10 miles from the Canadian border on the Kettle River. It was a beautiful community in a rustic sort of way.

Before leaving Alaska, I told Donna, "We have got to know this is God. We cannot trust our emotions on this one."

We proceeded to put together a fleece to know if this was God's will. The fleece was patterned after the scripture in Judges where Gideon needed to know if God had really called him to lead Israel. Gideon put down a sheep fleece and asked God to make the fleece dry and the ground wet if God was really calling him to lead Israel. To Gideon's surprise, God answered his request. But to be sure, he asked God to reverse the process the next night, and again God answered in the affirmative (Judges

6:36-40). Following this principle, we selected three things that only Donna and I would know and see how God would answer us. I then added two more that I didn't tell Donna about. This was a major move, and I had to know if it was God's leading and not an emotional one either to stay in Alaska or make the move to Orient.

The fleeces in order:

First: Knowing the area and knowing that there were no commercial places to stay within 20-30 miles, we said the church would have to provide us with a nice place to stay while in Orient. When we arrived, we were taken to an older furnished home that was empty. The home was clean and tidy, very comfortable, and close to the church. Number one answered.

Second: Knowing that the attendance was down to 12-15, we said we wanted at least 30 in attendance on our second Sunday. When Sunday arrived, I was stunned to find there were over 30 present and also over 30 for our second Sunday. Number two answered.

Third: Knowing that the Church was down, I felt that they were not in a position to offer any financial assistance for a move from Alaska to Orient. But they had to at least make some kind of offer. One of the first questions asked of us after our second Sunday was, "What do we have to do to get you to come?" Number three answered with "The Offer."

These were the fleeces Donna and I put out, and they were answered forthwith.

Fourth: One of the conditions that I added. Knowing Donna had never been to Orient and being from the city, it was important that she be happy with the small church and the rural community. As we were driving from Spokane north to Orient, she was wondering, "Where are we going?" The country became more and more rural. However, when we stepped inside the church for the first time, Donna lifted her hands and exclaimed, "I love it." Answer number four. One to go.

Fifth: It was important that the church in Palmer be good with our move. When we returned to Palmer, the pastor that we had helped to restore to full-time ministry met me and said, "I know you are going. When are you leaving?" To our amazement, all five fleeces were answered in rapid order: bam, bam, bam. Everything we asked God for made it clear that we were to move to Orient and be the pastors of the Orient Community Church.

Glen & Donna in front of welcome sign of Orient Community Church 2008

6:36-40). Following this principle, we selected three things that only Donna and I would know and see how God would answer us. I then added two more that I didn't tell Donna about. This was a major move, and I had to know if it was God's leading and not an emotional one either to stay in Alaska or make the move to Orient.

The fleeces in order:

First: Knowing the area and knowing that there were no commercial places to stay within 20-30 miles, we said the church would have to provide us with a nice place to stay while in Orient. When we arrived, we were taken to an older furnished home that was empty. The home was clean and tidy, very comfortable, and close to the church. Number one answered.

Second: Knowing that the attendance was down to 12-15, we said we wanted at least 30 in attendance on our second Sunday. When Sunday arrived, I was stunned to find there were over 30 present and also over 30 for our second Sunday. Number two answered.

Third: Knowing that the Church was down, I felt that they were not in a position to offer any financial assistance for a move from Alaska to Orient. But they had to at least make some kind of offer. One of the first questions asked of us after our second Sunday was, "What do we have to do to get you to come?" Number three answered with "The Offer."

These were the fleeces Donna and I put out, and they were answered forthwith.

Fourth: One of the conditions that I added. Knowing Donna had never been to Orient and being from the city, it was important that she be happy with the small church and the rural community. As we were driving from Spokane north to Orient, she was wondering, "Where are we going?" The country became more and more rural. However, when we stepped inside the church for the first time, Donna lifted her hands and exclaimed, "I love it." Answer number four. One to go.

Fifth: It was important that the church in Palmer be good with our move. When we returned to Palmer, the pastor that we had helped to restore to full-time ministry met me and said, "I know you are going. When are you leaving?" To our amazement, all five fleeces were answered in rapid order: bam, bam, bam. Everything we asked God for made it clear that we were to move to Orient and be the pastors of the Orient Community Church.

Glen & Donna in front of welcome sign of Orient Community Church 2008

January of 2006, we moved into our home in Orient, a lovely place on the river, and began our ministry. The church grew in numbers, and healing was brought to the church and community. I cannot express the joy we both enjoyed during our short stay there.

Life has a way of changing the directions we must take to follow God's plan for our lives. I believe God works in various ways to lead his children in different directions. Health issues became an issue for us because of the distance to medical facilities. As a result, we decided it best to resign the church and move. After two years in Orient, we made the difficult decision to relocate to Spokane, Washington where we already had medical connections.

Move To Spokane

I never cease to be amazed at how God provides for us. God had a place for us reserved in a nice neighborhood, close to medical, shopping, and church. This happened to be the first place we looked at, but we didn't make an offer at that time. For two months we drove about one thousand miles around Spokane looking for the right place only to come back to where we started. I might add that the price had dropped by about fifteen thousand dollars in that two month period. God is good. Our neighbors told us they were surprised that we got the home because there were a lot of lookers. I told them it was because God had been saving it for us.

Our home was close to where Alpha Omega Tours and Charters shop was located. After driving by for several weeks, I decided to see if they were interested in a part-time driver. Entering the office, I asked if they were interested in an experienced driver who didn't want to do very much. To my surprise, they said yes. As a result, I went to work on a part-time basis. This developed into an opportunity to travel with the owner as a helper on different tours. My job was to walk up and down the aisle of the bus passing out candy and snacks and visiting with the people. I also helped with luggage and drove when needed. I have had the privilege to travel from coast to coast, north to the south, and trips into Canada. Donna could travel with us if she desired and has gone on several trips. She especially enjoyed the trips to Branson, Missouri.

When we moved to Spokane, Donna and I church shopped for a few weeks and then attended the Spokane First Church of the Nazarene. We liked the church and discovered that the pastor was new to the church. I don't know if that had any influence on us, but we settled in and we enjoyed the worship and preaching.

After we became somewhat acquainted, I was asked if I would help teach an adult Sunday school class. I accepted on the basis that I would be a helper and not be the primary teacher. As time passed, the teacher moved from Spokane, and I found myself the teacher. The class was titled "Practical Christian Living." The suggested format was to discuss the pastor's sermon. However, we seldom followed that format. Instead, we often found ourselves in an open forum discussing the major needs and blessings of the class or what was on their hearts. From one Sunday to the next, I never knew for sure what would be discussed or what direction the class would take. What seemed to determine the subject was an individual need or what was on the class's heart. The class centered on what was the most needed to help with practical Christian living.

How to prepare for such a class had never been taught to me. I have never been in a situation like this before having taught different ages in different churches but always with a lesson plan. I really didn't have a plan to go by because the needs were so varied.

I came up with what I believed was a workable plan. I have devoted myself to reading a lot of books from different authors.

I read and studied the Scriptures and have given myself to daily prayer and worship. I knew of no other way to be prepared to answer questions and facilitate the class in a meaningful way to practical Christian living.

As I bring this writing to a close, I want anyone who may read this to know that I have not always lived a life of victory and total commitment to Christ. I have never turned away from God to my willful self without keeping at least a door open between the Lord and me. I have always been open to his call no matter what, when, or where it may be.

I would like to add this one thing: If you do not have a personal relationship with Jesus Christ, I encourage you to reach out and invite Jesus to be your personal Lord and Savior. God loves you as much as he loves me, and I know that God can fill your life with peace and contentment, giving you the only security that will stand the storms that are coming to our nation.

To God Be the Glory for All He Has Done.